SMUGGLING IN WEST ARGYLL AND LOCHABER

BEFORE 1745

COVER ILLUSTRATIONS

FRONT COVER - An early view of Oban Bay and the Sound of Kerrera seen from the Oban shore. Horseshoe Bay lies beyond the small Heather Island in the distance where two ships can be seen. (Artist unknown).
Reproduced with permission of Madam Morag MacDougall of Dunollie.

BACK COVER - Duart Castle on Mull. Detail from a plan by Paul Sandby in 1747.
Reproduced with permission of the Trustees of the National Library of Scotland.

SMUGGLING IN WEST ARGYLL & LOCHABER *Before 1745*

Charles Hunter

from the Archives at Ardchattan Priory

First Published 2004 by
Charles Hunter Publisher
Summit, Pulpit Hill, Oban, Argyll, PA34 4LX
01631 564876
E-mail obanch@aol.com

ISBN 0 9517230 3 0

Designed
by Alloway Publishing

Printed by
Walker & Connell Ltd
Hastings Square, Darvel, Ayrshire

By the same author:

OBAN - PAST AND PRESENT ISBN 0 9517230 2 2
OBAN - PREHISTORY (out of print)
OBAN, KILMORE AND KILBRIDE (out of print)

Introduction

Scotland in the early eighteenth century was a veritable hotbed of smuggling. New taxes imposed with the Union of 1707 and the employment of additional customs and excise officers trained to higher English standards were strongly resented. Places which before the Union had seen little in the way of officialdom now found that their trade was subject to rigorous rules and regulations – and financial impositions. As a result, not only was smuggling rife and condoned at the highest level, but officers were assaulted by braying mobs, often led by or involving, females armed with sticks and stones.

Charles Hunter's account of smuggling in west Argyll and Lochaber between 1725 and 1745 deals with the period when this activity was at its height. Merchants could make small fortunes by trading illegally, while the spoils of smuggling – even if this meant stopping state officials from carrying out their duties – percolated down to the lowest ranks. The poor benefited too from the lower prices they paid for tax-free goods.

This publication too deals with a part of the country that is often overlooked in studies of trade, commerce and industrial activity. But the west Highlands of Scotland had much to offer in the early eighteenth century. Ease of access by water was one advantage that allowed Welsh and English ironmasters to send iron ore by sea for smelting. Landowners like the earls of Breadalbane cultivated and leased out for felling extensive forests, with charcoal being the main fuel used by ironmasters prior to the age of coke which shifted manufacturing operations to Scotland's central belt. Slate too could be moved by sea, and was much in demand from the growing towns in the south, where timber and thatch were being replaced by stone buildings which were less vulnerable to fire and more fashionable.

This publication provides a vivid account of this and other economic activity in pre-industrial Scotland. Fishing had long been carried on in the western firths and lochs – with hundreds of boats being employed, mainly to serve the rising Glasgow market, although salted fish was also sought in the West Indies which were, after 1707, open to Scottish traders. This and other enterprises are brought to life here by the extensive use of quotations from primary sources, the documents from the period. Hitherto these, drawn from the collection at Ardchattan that covers the Inveresragan estate, have been little-used. Historians will be intrigued through this publication and will want to see the original, to add to and perhaps refine the initial analysis provided here by Charles Hunter; other readers will be fascinated by what they learn and understand better the history of a region that was at the heart of the economy of Scotland before the industrial revolution.

Professor Christopher A Whatley
Dean, Faculty of Arts and Social Sciences, University of Dundee

Charles Hunter, born in India of Scottish parents, was educated at Oban High School during the war years and at Sandhurst. After thirteen years in the Royal Engineers he took early retirement and worked in technical sales and marketing, based in London. In 1978 he and his wife returned to Oban when he became self-employed.

He has sons in Edinburgh and in California. His interests are local history, archaeology, photography and travel.

Acknowledgements

This is an account of sophisticated smuggling, illegal trading and sharp practice in a remote part of the Western Highlands of Scotland during the little-known period of the twenty years before the "Forty-five" Jacobite Rebellion. The story is told largely in the participants' own words, thanks to the survival of the remarkable business records preserved at Ardchattan Priory on Loch Etive, near Oban. The variations in spelling and punctuation, sometimes within the same manuscript, have been altered only slightly for the sake of clarity.

The text of this booklet has been compiled and edited from a verbatim record of about 100,000 words, which is now on disk to help future researchers. Much has been left out, notably the records of sales from the shop at Inveresragan and the names of petty traders and local customers throughout Lorn and the Inner Hebrides.

I am greatly indebted to Mrs Sarah Troughton of Ardchattan Priory for allowing me, over the past year or two, to examine the trading records of Inveresragan which have been preserved.

I would like to thank the managers, curators and staff of the following bodies for their help with references and illustrations. The Tate Gallery; The National Library of Scotland; the National Archives of Scotland; the National Maritime Museum; the Scottish Maritime Museum; the National Gallery of Scotland; the National Museum of Scotland; the Royal Commission; the Mitchell Library in Glasgow; the National Library of Wales and the Isle of Man Archives.
I would also like to thank the archivist of Argyll & Bute Council and curators of the West Highland Museum at Fort William, the Easdale Island Folk Museum and the Mull Museum. My personal thanks go to Madam Morag MacDougall of Dunollie, Frances Wilkins, Professor Michael Moss and Robert McBride of Alloway Publishing Ltd.

Finally I wish to thank Professor Christopher Whatley, Dean of the Faculty of Arts and Social Sciences at the University of Dundee, for his encouragement and for his generous Introduction.

Charles Hunter
2004

Illustrations

Contents

SMUGGLING IN
WEST ARGYLL & LOCHABER
before 1745

Earliest Trading in West Argyll and Lochaber

The earliest trading around Oban was with foreign fishermen who followed the herring shoals around the coast every summer. Herring and salmon were salted for sale to distant ports throughout the eighteenth century. Surplus cattle were driven to lowland markets, the earliest recorded at Oban being in 1622. Subsistence farming was the norm and the standard of living was low. Nationally by 1700 the Scots pound was worth only one-twelfth of the English pound sterling and in 1707 Union with England took place.

The positive results of the Union of the parliaments of England and Scotland were the removal of the monopolies enjoyed by the traders of Royal Burghs and the new freedom which allowed merchants in Scotland to trade legally with England and the English colonies. The only Royal burghs in the west of Scotland at that time, apart from those on the Ayrshire and Galloway coasts, were Glasgow with its satellite ports of Greenock and Port Glasgow, and Renfrew, Dumbarton, Rothesay, Inveraray and Campbeltown in Kintyre.
The downside of the Union was the imposition of the English system of Customs and Excise, which was more efficient than the earlier regime. The principal Customs posts for Glasgow were the Headport at Newport Glasgow and at Greenock. Soon after the Union a Customs Post was set up at the Garrison of Fort William to supervise the sea and land as far south as Tarbert, while another Post at Campbeltown covered southern Kintyre. To keep the peace in West Argyll there were military Garrisons at Fort William, at Duart Castle on Mull and later at Kilchurn Castle on Loch Awe.

During the eighteenth century Scottish landowners formed alliances with entrepreneurs to exploit the natural resources of the Highlands, especially slate, lead, granite and timber. Workers were paid wages in cash at about one shilling Sterling per day. This created a demand for the consumer products of the industrial revolution, and for stimulants such as alcohol, tobacco and tea.

The granting of timber rights by Sir Duncan Campbell 7th of Lochnell, the second Earl of Breadalbane and others dates from 1721-23. This trade was mainly in fir timber for an Irish company, which was also setting up an ironworks at Glenkinglas on the remote north-eastern shore of Loch Etive. Iron smelting, using oak charcoal as fuel, had started by 5th February 1725 and continued at least to 18th November 1732. (RCAHMS).

There are indications in the Ardchattan archives, from persons named in the Inveresragan shop day books, that the ironworks may have still been in production as late as 1741.　　(appendix C).

Loch Etive in Lorn

The shores of Loch Etive in Argyll seem an unlikely place for trade by land or by sea. Life there centred on Ardchattan Priory, a monastery built in 1230 AD, which came into secular Campbell ownership after the Reformation of 1560. The seven-merk land of Inveresragan lay east of the Priory and adjoined Ardchattan lands. The secretive inlet at Bonawe, on the north shore of Loch Etive is three miles east of Ardchattan. The excellent harbour there is used to this day by the owners of Bonawe Quarry. When anchored there, the masts of a sailing ship would hardly be seen from any other part of the loch. However the main settlement of Bonawe was on the south shore of Loch Etive, near where the new ironworks were built after the "Forty-five". (Illustrated).

By 1730 the "Glenkinglas timber company in Glenorchy" had a sawmill at Bonawe. Apparently fir logs were floated down the River Orchy when in spate, through Loch Awe, then down the River Awe to Loch Etive. (Wormell).

Captain Arthur Galbraith of Dublin was manager of the Firwood Company at Bonawe and Alexander Campbell was his clerk. Fir and oak timber was put to a wide variety of flooring, building and marine uses. Oak was also converted into charcoal over a very wide area to fuel the furnace at Glenkinglas. There was a company at Bonawe to supply meal to the Glenkinglas workers and also a fishing company to process salmon and herring. Sir Duncan Campbell of Lochnell was prominent in all of these ventures. In addition the Bonawe granite quarries may have been started because three quarriers are named in the Inveresragan shop day-books before 1745. The lead mines at Strontian on Loch Sunart were also partly supplied from Bonawe.

There was a ferry crossing at Bonawe and a second ferry crossed Loch Etive at Connel near the narrow turbulent entrance, below to-day's century-old iron bridge. Dunstaffnage Bay with its 13th century

Castle lies to the west outside Loch Etive. (Illustrated p. 97)
Oban Bay, whose entrance is overlooked by Dunollie Castle, is two miles further west. (Illustrated p. 104)
The island of Kerrera almost encloses Oban Bay and some way down the Sound of Kerrera, a sheltered harbour called "Horse-shoe Anchorage" was described by the Royal Navy during the 1745-6 Rebellion as "a fine safe little harbour". (Gibson).
In the trading records this bay was usually called "the horse shoe". (Illustrated p. 17/18)
Duart Castle and the mountains of Mull and Morvern are on the far side of the wide Firth of Lorn. (Illustrated p.99)
The low-lying island of Lismore stretches along the centre of the Firth towards Appin and Fort William. (Illustrated)
All of these places feature in the Inveresragan trading records at Ardchattan Priory. (appendix D)

Coline Campbell of Inveresragan

The Inveresragan records run from 1720 and end with the death of Coline Campbell of Inveresragan in late May or early June 1745.
The earliest papers have little to do with trading or smuggling. They were letters about farming and rural concerns or legal disputes over trifling sums of Scots money. Two documents dating back to 1720 give an indication firstly of Coline Campbell of Inveresragan's standing as a loyal gentleman landowner and secondly of his wide range of interests in religion, literature and politics. A list of books purchased from Mr Alexander Symmer of Edinburgh dates back to August 1721 and includes Plutarch's Lives in five volumes, works by Congreave and Dryden, various religious tracts and "Montroses Wars". (Illustrated p. 15)

Coline was certainly not a Jacobite sympathiser, because he was one of two landowners ordered, in 1720, by the Honourable James Campbell of Stonefield, Deputy Chief Justice of Argyll and the Western Isles, to "seize and apprehend several persons, strangers, who have lately past through Inverara and appeard to be highly Disaffected to His Majestys Person and Government". They were "Lately Come from Spain to carry on Indirect practices against the Government" and were undoubtedly stragglers from the1719 Spanish landing. There is no further reference to this affair. (Illustrated p. 14)

There are remarkably few personal references in the trading correspondence but it appears that Coline was a widower, having been married to a niece of Sir James Campbell of Ardkinglas on Loch Fyne. He had a son James – who was a young adult by 1745 - and a daughter Margaret. Coline is presumed to have died between 28th

At the Honourable James
Campbell of Stonefield Esquire Deputy
Chief Justice of the County of Argyll and
western Isles of Scotland and of all Land
Belonging Either in Property or Superiority
To the Duke of Argyll within Scotland And
on of the Deputy Lievtenants and Justices of
Peace of the said County

Whereas There is and Information Given in to me
Setting forth that Severall persons have Lately past through
Inverara who Appeard to be highly Disaffected to his Majes-
=ties Person and Government And by Severall Concurring
Circumstances And shewed by the foresaid Information as
given in to me Appear to be Lately Come from Spain as
to Carry on Indirect practises against the Government
These are Therefore Giving full power warrand and
Commission To Argus Campbell of Askmish And Collin
Campbell of Inveresrogan and Such as they shall
imploy to seize and Apprehend the fornamed persons
or any of them that can be found with any papers
Cash or any other Suspected thing that Can be found
about them and to bring them prisoners to Inverara
Requiring hereby all his Majestys Lidges to be Assist-
=ing to them for putting the forsaid warrand In Execution
In Testimony whereof these presents are Signed and Sealed
at Inverara The fourteenth Day of February one thousand
Seven hundred and twenty and of his Majestys Reign
the Sixth Year with power where to press horses for
payment of the ordinary hire In any place within the
said Jurisdiction

A 1720 Warrant authorising Coline Campbell of Inveresragan to arrest Spanish soldiers who had landed in 1719 to support the Jacobites. © *Ardchattan Priory Archives.*

Mr Collin Campbell of Inverstregan

owe To Mr Alexander Symmet Bookseller £ s d

To montrous wars	0	3 0
first Gamester	0	1 8
Hubrichs lines 5 Vol	0	18 0
Derhams Physico theology	0	6 0
Warden on bees	0	1 8
Browns letters	0	2 6
Bishes Art of Poetry	0	5 6
Gentlemans Library	0	4 0
Congreves works 4 Vol	0	7 6
Popes miscelanys	0	16 0
Butlers Posthumous works	0	3 0
2 plays viz Ulysses & Hamlet	0	2 0
Derhams Astro theology	0	5 0
Pelrinus arbiter	0	3 0
Presbeterian Eloquence	0	2 4
Prideaux Conections 2 Vol	0	16 0
Woolstones discoursing	0	6 0
Dictionarum Buchian	0	7 6
Caswlion of Protest	0	1 0
Sinnets theory 2 Vol	0	13 0
Prideaux life of Mahomet	0	3 0
Virtuts Discoveries of Rome 2 Vol	0	11 0
the ruling cleer	0	0 3
another scope of virtues discoveries	0	11 0
Pichindrums Dictionar	0	7 6
Tryal of Virtues	0	5 0
Remarks on Burnet	0	1 8
Masqueraders	0	1 2
Spirit of Ecclesiasticks	0	1 2
To a three int him	0	1 2½
Rights of Assem church	0	6 0
Immortal Passion	0	0 2
the fifes letter	0	0 2
To hee and hixion	0	2 4
bringer independent whig	0	4 0
carried over	8	15 3¾

Brought over	8	15 3¾
To grounds of their Religion	0	6 0
Coventrys Answer to Do	0	6 0
Free thoughts on Religion	0	5 0
	9	12 3¾

Contra Cred

By Cash	2	0 0
By Ditto	1	1 0
By Ditto from Mr McVicll	1	0 0
By	0	10 0
By	0	6 6
By Do from Mr Bahay	3	9 9
med Ballince	3	5 6

Edr March 2. 1731
Received from Mr Campbell of Inveraw the payment of
the above Accompt and discharges the same and all pre
ceedings ... Symmet

Coline Campbell's booklist from Edinburgh, 1720-26. © Ardchattan Priory Archives.

15

May and 5th June 1745. He was succeeded by James, who was unable to continue the business. Shortly afterwards the Inveresragan lands were adjoined to Ardchattan and on 26th August 1747 James Campbell of Inveresragan was admitted a Burgess of Inveraray as "Ensign in Inverawe's Company". (Burgesses of Inveraray)

There are many boxes of manuscript records at Ardchattan filed in 1957 by the Scottish Record Office under the general title of "Loch Etive Trading Company". Only the eleven boxes which encompass Inveresragan have been examined. (appendix D)

A small section of the Inveresragan records include details of another merchant, identified only as "P.C." He was, at least from 1743-45, trading successfully and separately at Ardchattan in partnership with east coast merchants and had no apparent link with Inveresragan. (Historic Argyll No 8, 2003)

The Lochetty Company

From his remote outpost near Bonawe, Coline Campbell of Inveresragan sold tobacco, in rolls of 10-15 pounds weight to packmen and small traders, at about ninepence to tenpence per pound Sterling. The earliest date in Coline Campbell's lists of debtors was for a roll of tobacco sold locally on 11th May 1723. He also bottled for local sale wine and brandy bought in casks from well-known merchant smugglers such as John Somervell of Renfrew and Bailie John Steuart of Inverness. He bought tobacco and wines from James Fisher of Inveraray, whose earliest account, priced in Scots money, was dated 15th April 1726.

On 15th May 1728 Coline Campbell formed a trading partnership called the Lochetty Company with three other local Campbell landowners. They were John Campbell of Barcaldine, John Campbell of Lossit in Kintyre and Duncan Campbell of Inverawe. Coline was appointed manager, initially at £33 Sterling per annum and latterly at a salary of £40 per annum, plus expenses.

Coline Campbell's first "waste book" of expenses, written in his own hand, shows that he tackled his new responsibilities with vigour. For example he noted during 1728:

6th June: "bought 6 hogsheads of claret for £39 from James Cathcart of Ayr at Clachan Seil".

24th July: "bought a cask of brandy for £45-15s from Bailie Steuart of Inverness, then in Kinlochaber".

10th October: "bought 10¾ gallons of rum from Duncan Campbell in Lergyvullin in Islay, which was brought to Dunstaffnage".

In each case, Coline Campbell had to arrange freight from the point of purchase to Bonawe or to his cellars at Inveresragan.

20th December: "Spent with Mr John Somervell making bargains for the Company".

We can be fairly sure that all these bargains were of dutiable goods shipped for export and relanded duty-free and illegally by the sellers in the remote places named above.

The Customs duty could be reclaimed on goods cleared for export. If these could be relanded undetected by Customs, a large profit would be made.

During 1729 Coline Campbell's stated expenses included:

23rd March: "going to Mull, freighting a ship to Kerrera where I was stormbound for three days in Pattrick McGrigars house in Oban". The details of this transaction are given in a note and a bill signed by John Somervell Junior on 23rd March at Kerrera:

"Delivered to Coline Campbell of Inveresragan at Kerrera:

256 gallons brandy at 13s 4d per gallon £170-13-4d

6 hogsheads claret at £8 per hhd   £ 48

2 hogsheads white wine at £7 per hhd   £ 14"

The bill orders: "Coline Campbell & company: Pay to me ...six months after (this) date at the coffee house in Glasgow: £232-13-4d Sterling".

14th April: "spent with Mr Somervell in buying 4 hogsheads, 2 at 4 pence per lib (pound) & 2 inland later at the Lump price deliverable here". This is the first mention of tobacco being bought in bulk and at a duty-free price. A hogshead of leaf tobacco weighed 600-800 pounds, depending on the size of the barrel, but these purchases would have been of rolled tobacco.

9th July: "purchased from Mr Somervell 6 gross bottles and corks and freighted them from Dunstaffnidge to Inveresragan".

13th July: "with Mr Somervell at the Garrison (Fort William) endeavouring to buy 40 bolls of meall with him".

22nd August: "went to Kengerloch (Kingairloch in Morvern on the remote north shore of Loch Linnhe) to meet John Somervell to buy a 5 tunn brandy, 1 hhd claret and 2 of white wine". This involved "freighting the boat of Shian with two hands" and the hire of another three hands.

17th September: Coline spent a night at Bonawe with John Somervell when paying a due debt of £40-15s.

On 10th December 1729 John Somervell wrote from Glasgow to Coline Campbell at Inveresragan: "Expected to have seen you myself but my father being indisposed cannot see you before January. All your affairs are on board of the *Robert Ramsay* but the wind being so much out of the way and the weather so bad she cannot sail.

Pray give my service to Inveraw and tell him his brother sailed from

64
m

57

soufflé

KERFERRY

Ilanakine

Illangaun

Olatrach

Barnaback

Ferry

Ardendrach

Glensfrilach

KILBR

Bachk

Dupore

66
m

45
m

L. Euchan

47
m

Bewackery

Dupore

Harindrone

Ardintallin

Kilnore

Inish

Kilninver

Swandirmik

Clachan Seil

Dunmore

SUIL I.

Fyfsil I.

NETHER LORN

Balabua

Ardmaddy

Melfort

Torsa I.

Kilchoan

Ardista

Black Harbour

L. Melfort

LOING I.

Ilan-nagaus

Cairnsmichel

Ardernish

Parift

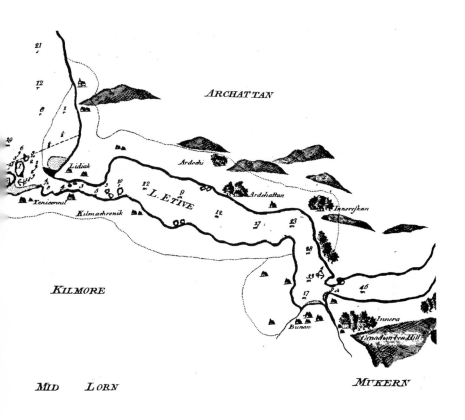

A detail from "West Coast of Scotland from Ila to Mull", a chart by Murdoch Mackenzie published in 1776 but surveyed earlier. Bonawe, Inveresragan, Dunstaffnage, Oban and Horseshoe Bay are all shown. © Crown Copyright.
Reproduced by permission of the Trustees of the National Library of Scotland.

Pert Henry in Ireland for the Canaries about 20 days ago and was very well. (signed) John Somervell".

In the only known letter from Bailie John Steuart of Inverness, he signs his name as "Steuart" with a flourish at either end but no initials. The letter, addressed to Coline Campbell on 4th September 1730 from "Mary Burgh"- the village at Fort William - reads:
"I had Sir Duncan Campbells promise not long since that he would order you payment and I now write to him in the most pressing terms I can. I'm hopeful youll recover paytt of the others I left with you and I begg it with all earnestness and as a singular favour that youll lend me your assistance. Your Brother promised he would be cleared before this time. Inveraw I'm persuaded will not be wanting in his which youll see by the Book what it amounts to. I came home the other day from Inverness and my Spouse is much Indisposed so that I cannot come so soon to your country as I could incline".
(GD 1 / 2 9/4)
Sir Duncan Campbell of Lochnell was the principal landowner in Lorn and was at that time fully involved in the ironworks at Glenkinglas on Loch Etive, in fir timber extraction, and with fishing and meal companies. Campbell of Inverawe was the next most important landowner in Lorn. Coline's brother Archibald, mentioned above, was the postmaster at Inveraray and also an inn keeper there. (postal records at Appendix C)
It seems that everybody owed money to Bailie Steuart.

Bailie Steuart's Letterbook shows that his main business was supplying meal legally from the East Coast of Scotland to the West. He supplied the Garrisons at Fort William and at Duart and the lead mines at Strontian and on Skye. This was shipped round the north of Scotland or down Loch Ness and then overland with a military escort. He was strongly opposed to the import of cheap duty-free meal from Ireland, but smuggling of wines and spirits was a lucrative sideline, often to his legal meal customers. He was a Jacobite sympathiser and an Episcopalian but this never got in the way of business! By 1730 Bailie Steuart was nearing the end of his active career which foundered because of extended credit and unpaid bills. On one speculative voyage of his ship, the *Christian*, to Skye he instructed his skipper to sail afterwards to Stornoway for cash sales but to "trust no one there". He spent the last years of his long life in penury, cared for by his large family from two marriages. (Steuart Letterbook)

William Fogo of Kilhorn
Glasgow, with a population of about 20,000, had only been a Royal Burgh since 1690 when its first quay at the Broomilaw was only two

years old. The River Clyde was extremely shallow and was described as being "in a state of nature" as late as 1755. Exports and imports were handled through Greenock or the new port built on 13 acres near Greenock, to enable Glasgow merchants to compete with English merchants in Bristol, Liverpool and Whitehaven.
Before 1730, no great fortunes had been made by the tobacco merchants of Glasgow. Scottish trade with England and the English colonies had only been legal since 1707, and was strongly opposed by English merchants. The Scottish merchants of this little-known period included the brothers William and Henry Fogo.

William Fogo of Kilhorn (Killearn) was an experienced tobacco merchant with premises in Glasgow. He married Barbara, daughter of the late Provost of Glasgow, John Anderson of Dowhill, who had died in 1710. Barbara's marriage settlement on 9th February 1731 included half of her late father's lands, which comprised about six acres of virtually unbuilt land.at Dowhill on Glasgow's Gallowgate. Her sister Marion, by Mary Hay, John Anderson's second wife, inherited the other half. (Glasgow, Past & Present) (Dell, SRO B10/15/6503). John's first wife was Susanna Hamilton, who may have been related to Thomas Hamilton, Chirurgeon and late Bailie of Glasgow, who was in partnership in November 1729 with John Mitchell, William & Henry Fogo and George Thomson.   (Dell, SRO B 10/15/4152)
William Fogo was involved in several partnerships, which were sometimes formed to share the responsibility of bonding single tobacco cargoes at the appropriate Customs House.

The earliest Fogo transaction to appear in the records at Ardchattan Priory is a bond of £400- 9- 8 sterling for duty payable on 21,202 lbs of leaf tobacco imported from Virginia in the *Agnes* of Glasgow, Archibald Stewart, Master. This was "entered at Port Glasgow on 23rd September 1724 by William and Henry Fogo and others". In the same year an unnamed brigantine was clearing for export of tobacco from the Clyde to Guernsey.

There must surely have been some early connection here between Coline Campbell and the Fogo brothers for these 1724 records to be in the Inveresragan files in the Ardchattan Priory archive.
It is known that James Graham (1/2), John Campbell (1/4) and William Fogo (1/4) were partners in a cargo of the ship *Agnes* in 1726.
                              (Dell, SRO B10/15/4436)

William Fogo replaced John Campbell of Barcaldine as a partner of the Lochetty Company on 19th February 1730. Copies of letters sent by Coline Campbell show how this was done.   (GD/1/2/15/206)
An 18th February letter to Duncan Campbell of Inverawe reads: "Met

Mr Fogo at Inveraray and settled with him as to Barcaldine's share. Lossit and I are to meet Barcaldine to get a right to his ¼ share. We are lucky to have Mr Fogo engaged".

On 21st February to William Fogo: "On 19th inst we settled with Barcaldine. Got a right to his share and accepted a bill for £56 & £14 sterling which he owed".

9th March to Mr Fogo: "You'll owe Lossit £56 and the Company £14".

The partnership of Messrs William & Henry Fogo and John Mitchell is recorded at Ardchattan as having imported listed "Dutch goods" to the high value of £2,204 – 7s sterling from Rotterdam to Greenock in the *Mary & Jean*, George Dennie Master. Alexander Naughten, of Rotterdam invoiced these on 18th October 1730. Some of these Dutch goods were sold to the Lochetty Company by William Fogo.

(GD1/2/17 1-2/1).

Some tobacco from the 1730 voyage of the *Fame* from Virginia may also have found its way to Inveresragan, where a tobacco mill was built during 1730 with encouragement and help from William Fogo.

Two letters dated 18th February 1730, written by Coline Campbell, appear to confirm the start of tobacco milling at Inveresragan. One to Duncan Campbell of Inverawe, a partner in the Lochetty company, reads: "Our goods from Clyde arrived last week. Our presses from Inveraray I hope are now at Branry (Brander), so will commence the tobacco spinning immediately". The other letter, to William Fogo, reads: "After I parted with you at Carricks, went to Inveraray and sent off two of the presses for my house. The two hogsheads from Clyde are safely arrived".

(GD1/2/15/206)

We know that John Brown, tobacco spinner and burgess of Inveraray, was at Inveresragan in February 1730, presumably to set up the tobacco mill there. Another tobacco spinner and burgess of Inveraray, Philip Innes, arrived before the end of the year.

(Burgesses of Inveraray)

Robert Arthur's Early Ventures

On 27th February 1730 William Fogo wrote to Coline Campbell that he intended sending Mr Arthur the next week. This fixes the position of the following undated letter sent to Coline Campbell and copied to John Campbell of Lossit and Company.

"I have sent the ten hhds by the bearer Robert Arthur. Because of dear freight for such a small tool of a ship, besides the risk I run, have made out the account to £129-13s-5¼d at 3¾d (per lb). If he delivers you the other ten you'll stow them in a convenient place till further orders, but if you can dispose of any of them at 4d per lb you may do it on my account. I can assure you good tobacco is scarce. Write me when it comes to hand under the name of meal. The bearer goes for Norway so give him any commissions for iron ... and in case he brings you brandy or any other things you are to receive them and charge them to my account in your book". The final invoice for the ten hogsheads of tobacco was £126-10s-3d sterling for 8,376 lbs.

On 17th April 1730 Mr Fogo wrote: " I understand that my friend may deliver the meal before this time. Desire you keep all matter quiet. Dispatch him without loss of time because the (Customs) yacht is out ... in quest of him ...act cautiously for fear of your neighbours giving Information. I am advised that he was to leave money with you. If he has gone return it by the bearer and dispatch him without loss of time ... uneasy till I hear from you".

This first visit of Robert Arthur to Inveresragan on Loch Etive was noted in Coline Campbell's expenses book on 21st April 1730. It reads "then received 10 hogsheads tobacco from Mr William Fogo, merchant in Glasgow, by the hands of Mr Robert Arthur in Crawfords Dyke. Weight 8376 pounds which I accepted with an obligement and accepted Mr Fogos Draught at prime cost".

The next day Robert Arthur handed over £100 sterling in cash to Coline Campbell from Mr Fogo, as a result of which William Fogo became a full partner in the Lochetty Company.

The ten hogsheads delivered by Robert Arthur, who was then discribed as "William Fogo's Skipper", would have been the first bulk delivery of leaf tobacco to be rolled at Inveresragan.

Leading up to this first visit by Robert Arthur, the correspondence between Mr Fogo and Coline Campbell makes it clear that the ten hogsheads – and ten more which may have been dropped off at the same time - were part of a cargo sent for export and duty-free to Norway. If duty of more than 4d per pound had been paid for inland sale, the price to Coline Campbell would have been in the region of 8d per pound. Mr Fogo wrote: "Tobacco now advances to 8½d so be cautious in selling what you have on hand".

During 1730 leaf tobacco was also delivered to Inveresragan in other ships, namely:

5½ hogsheads by charter dated 26 October 1730 in the *Sea Flower* of Creills, Andrew Breudie Master. And there was another undated delivery of 3 hogsheads.

Robert Arthur also landed 22 casks of brandy at Bonawe for William Fogo, to be concealed at Inveresragan until required. Mr Fogo wrote to Coline on 5th June 1730 from "Loch how (Lochawe) head: I got here about three o clock and have agreed with Letter (Campbell of Letterawe?) to carry the twenty casks brandy from Bonawe to

Strathfillan. Hope you'll deliver them to him in good order at Bonawe on any day he shall appoint. Debit me with the charges and deliver the bearer two casks on his own account. Pray be careful to get the hoops secured. By Robert Campbell send me word of the day my men are to be at Strathfillan. Send the enclosed to John Campbell (of Lossit.) Desire you sell off none of the brandy under eighteen pence". On 17th June he wrote to Coline "See to deliver 20 casks of brandy to Robert Campbell as soon as possible: but if you can sell it you can keep the whole at 18 pence per pint and martinmas to pay".

William Fogo was introducing Coline to his friends in the wine and brandy trade. In May 1730 he recommended Messrs George and Robert Finsly (?) and John Black at Bordeaux. And on 29th June he mentions Mr Falconer, merchant in Edinburgh, who wished to land 2 tons of strong claret, ½ ton of wine and 2 tons of white wine at Kinlochaline, Lettershuna or Bonawe.

On 3rd August Mr Fogo wrote to Coline Campbell: "Desire you deliver to the bearer John McArthur 3 loads of my brandie ... keep account of the number of the casks you run and lay by ... beg the favour of your man to put them to Bonawe". On 10th August John McArthur the Carrier signed for 18 gallons and 1 pint of brandy.

In August 1730 there was an overland delivery from Bonawe through Strathfillan, in which Fort William merchant Mr Crawford was involved. William Fogo wrote on 3rd August: "Mr Crawford will be with your friend at the beginning of next month so be in readiness to answer his demands. You must employ some man of character to attend it and to come on with the horses till I meet them. Deliver the enclosed to Mr Crawford when (he) appears. Wish you may be on your guard lest the Customs of Fort William should have orders to watch you or Mr Crawford".

On 13th August 1730 Mr Fogo wrote to Coline Campbell:
"Clear out Mr Arthur ... if you can get it delayed and serve yourself otherwise it will be a singular favour and I shall allow it in part payment of your first bill, which will soon be due. Say what goods you want from the other place he is to touch at (so) that I may write to my factor. Also receive from (Mr Arthur) some small casks to empty the big casks into and cause carry them to Strathfillan to McNabs. All this (is) to be done as soon as possible and as quietly as you can". On 20th August Robert Arthur delivered 21 small casks for Mr Fogo's brandy to Bonawe.

On 16th October Mr Fogo wrote to Coline Campbell: "Shall endeavour to get down that brandie as soon as possible. Tell Mr Campbell to put it in small casks and to write how many horses it will need. On 29th October Mr Fogo wrote: "Carrier McArthur is to bring down what brandy remains, emptied into small casks and lying at Letters house where he is to receive it".

On 20th November 1730 John Campbell of Lossit, who was with Mr Fogo at the time, wrote to Coline; "My good brother Archie goes your length to get down Mr Arthur's things with as much secrecy as possible. Mr Fogo expects a good deal of money from you by Archie. If my broyr does not give you twenty pounds upon my account you may draw a bill upon me for the same. I suppose Mr Arthur is to be loaded with timber so that you'll do well to load him with the fir that you are to get from Glenkinglas Company, which will pay so much of your bill to Mr Fogo".

At Bonawe in November Robert Arthur loaded a cargo of fir timber for William Fogo to the value of £29- 8s. Mr Fogo wrote to Coline Campbell on 30th November: "I have advice this day that the (Customs) yacht sailed on Friday last for Lochaber ... they design to meet your friend. It was surmised that there was tobacco landed in the highlands and other goods. Would have you be on your guard ... if it comes your length ... carry any goods you have to some safe place. If your friend be not gone, fall on the best method to get him safely out lest the yacht be waiting him as he comes to sea. A warned man is half armed. Commit this to the flames. If questioned you can depone before a Justice that you believed the duty was paid, your friend selling it to you at 7½d per pound".

On his next visit to Bonawe on 11th January 1731 Robert Arthur personally collected money owed by Coline Campbell, namely £50 for William Fogo and £26-14s-6d for goods supplied by himself. Mr Arthur was already trading on his own account by this time, notably in snuff-making equipment.

William Fogo and his brother Henry both signed a letter to Coline Campbell on 22nd June 1731 about a consignment of tobacco: "We will deliver 15 hhds leaf tob: to you at Dunstaffnage at 4½d per pound". This was certainly a relanding.

On 23rd June 1731, William Duncan gabbartman was paid 10s by Coline "for carrying his goods from ye Broom of Law to North-barr". The receipt was signed "WD his mark".
"Nota: Baily Somervell abated 5s of his share of the freight to ye company".
Tobacco and other goods from the East of Scotland were often transferred to the Clyde ports overland to the Broomilaw and down the

River Clyde in shallow-draft gabbarts.

Coline Campbell's expenses were noted as £1-13- 5½ and the account was sent to James Hall in Greenock. Coline Campbell later claimed expenses of 12s for incidentals with James Lang, Collector and Ralph Bell, Comptroller of Customs at Greenock.

On 13th November 1731 Mr Fogo wrote: "our friend was waiting for favourable winds on 14th October to sail from the north". He hoped "he will be at your part very soon".

A massive cargo of 400 hogsheads of leaf tobacco was carried across the Atlantic by the *Fame* in 1731. Mr Fogo had an interest in this cargo, which was entered at a Clyde port.

Of this total, twenty hogsheads weighing 15,795 lbs were delivered to Inveresragan on 22nd May 1732 in James Beaton's gabbart for legal inland sale. The value at a duty-paid price of 7¼d per pound was £493-0-11 sterling. Coline Campbell paid £433 and was later told of his mistake by William Fogo, who demanded the balance of £60-0-11d .in a peremptory note. (GD 1/ 2 17 10/4)

The *Unity* delivered 6,226 lbs of leaf tobacco to Fort William from the same cargo. Of the total, about 7,000 lbs were exported, leaving 15,000 lbs in the Customs House at that time.

On 22nd December 1732 Mr Fogo reported that he "was at Greenock entering the *Diamond*". Twenty hogsheads weighing 14,085 lbs were delivered to Inveresragan from the *Diamond*'s 1732 cargo on 6th August 1733.

This was the ship which was to be most closely associated with Robert Arthur's early career, and he may have been on board.for his first trans-Atlantic voyage on this occasion. On 27th March 1731 Mr Fogo had written to Coline that "Arthur is now clear to sail for New England". Robert Arthur was then a young man, aged about thirty.

Exports to Ireland

Coline Campbell was supplying meal and shop goods to the Irish company whose ironworks was at Glenkinglas on the northeast shore of Loch Etive. On 8th March 1731, making use of this informal connection, he paid "20 guineas to Charles Coyle (manager) at the furnace to be employed in (importing) sundry goods at Dublin".

Following the setting up of the tobacco mill at Inveresragan the Lochetty Company partners decided to export tobacco to Ireland.

On 2nd June 1731 William Fogo instructed Coline to get a debenture in his own name from Fort William for 2-4,000 lbs of roll tobacco. In the same letter he wrote "the *Agnes* Gabbart is to sail for Dublin next week with coals and tobacco and is to return to Easdale there to be loaded with slate and if not then timber the best sort well squared. Write on Monday for making the slate ready".

The partners received detailed advice about the legal aspects of export to Ireland on 17th June 1731 from Will Tennoch, Writer in Edinburgh.

On 26th June 1731, 4,000 lbs of roll tobacco were exported from Fort William to Londonderry in the *Thomas* of Maryburgh, John Gibson Master. The tobacco leaf had been imported into Port Glasgow on 21st January 1730 in the *Margareen*, Richard Kelsick Master, and was presumably rolled at Inveresragan. Mr Fogo's instructions to Coline Campbell on this occasion were that "no part was to be landed in Great Britain or the Isle of Man".

There is an undated note of an export in 1731 of 16 hogsheads of leaf tobacco from Greenock to Thomas Stirling, Agent in Dublin. It has the reference "outward no. 672" and the ship was the *Providence* of Gourock, about 22 tons, with William Hasty Master and a crew of three. Only ships of over 20 tons could trade legally with Ireland.

Meanwhile the Lochetty Company continued to deal with other merchants and on 27th May 1731 Coline Campbell was "making bargain with George Douglas for the year for tobacco". In June Coline received a bill for £30- 7- 8 ½ from George Douglas, "merchant in Edinburgh but of Maryburgh". On 9th June Coline accepted a bill from Thomas Clark, merchant, for £60- 7- 8. This was "to be paid at the new coffee house in Glasgow". (GD1 / 2 /17 10/2) On 1st July a "docketted account" for £110- 1- 2 due to Mr John Somervell from the company, was settled by a cash payment of £10- 1- 2 and a promise to pay £100 Sterling at the end of August. On 21st July Thomas Hyndman in Newport (Glasgow) came to offer a cargo of tobacco.

On 23rd July 1731 Coline claimed £2-12 expenses for 8 days "going to Maryburgh re Export and our last Cachett with 3 hhds tobacco". The Collector was paid 12s 6d for the cash part of the Cachett.

On 7th January 1732, Mr Fogo wrote to Coline; "for export buy a dozen hhds and take it coastways. Go to Ireland with the roll and sell it to good men. Your note enclosed with Mr Arthur is long due and the 2 hhds your brother had the proceeds is never remitted though you said he had it readie. The Dutch goods are also due and the cask of brandie left at Bonawe". On 26th January he wrote: "Ship off 4000 libs and consign it to an honest man in Belfast – Mr Arbuckle or any other".
On 9th February 1732 Mr Fogo wrote to Coline: "I am very willing to

give the company and you advice and assistance and provide tobacco as well as any others provided you pay in due time which you yet never have done. Export to Norway is not difficult provided you can get a ship". And on 11th February he assured Coline "I shall provide you in good tobacco. I am still of the opinion that you export first to Ireland which will establish your character and give you a good grace".

On 24th February 1732 the *Diligence* of Irvine loaded a cargo for export. (GD1/ 2 12 20).   Captain Arthur Galbraith, manager of the Firwood Company at Bonawe, was at Inveresragan on 29th February 1732. He and Robert King of the *Diligence* were involved in a joint venture with Coline Campbell for the sale of fir timber to Robert Hunter. Robert King and the *Diligence* made several visits to Bonawe around this time and timber wasn't the only cargo he carried.
On 3rd March 1732 Coline instructed Robert King to deliver "12 Turses roll tobacco, which weighed 3,856 lbs, to Mr Arbuckle in Belfast, and to return with meal".   (GD 1 / 2 15/206).
The import of meal from Ireland to Scotland was illegal. On the same day Robert King's ship was loaded with the tobacco at Dunstaffnage for Belfast, supervised by the Customs Surveyor for fees of £5 and £1-2s. A second voyage that year took Robert King and the *Diligence* to Dublin with 6 hogsheads of tobacco.
The account dated 4th May for the first voyage was as follows:
    "Account of Coline Campbell of Inveresragan & Robert King
    to 60 tons of fir timber belonging to Capt Galbraith to which
    Inver has right of assignation   £63 - 0 - 0 (comprising)
    by due by Inver   £21 - 16 - 6
    due by Capt Galbraith   £18 - 8
    bill on John Campbell at Connel£ 5
    by cash received   £17 - 15 - 6 =   £63 - 0 - 0"
On the same day, at Connel, Coline Campbell paid Robert King £20-8-8 sterling for "Robert King's charges in Dublin and Belfast about the tob: and charges for entering ship for export tobacco". There is a reference to this £63, still unpaid, on 17th May 1733.
                                        (GD 1 /2 17 1-2/1)
However there seemed to be a problem with the voyages to Ireland. On 22nd May 1732 Mr Fogo wrote to Coline Campbell: "You have Mr Arbuckle's letter about the tobacco which will fright you from that mercate".

On 19th June 1732 Coline wrote in his expenses book: "Then granted receipt to my Broyr for 7½ Guineas for Bill for £6-2-11½ of Capt Galbraith".

On 20th August 1732 Mr Fogo was worried about a problem he shared with Robert Arthur and Coline Campbell. He wrote from Killorn to

Coline   "That unluckie affair has disconcerted matters.   Some exportation must be made to clear you of a part of that debt. There is one absolute necessity for you to provide a ship from Ayr or Irvine". On 4th September 1732 Mr Fogo wrote to Coline: "advise you that the tobacco must be exported immediately. Get a bark and ship it off or go to the coast side and freight one. There is such strong suspicion of frauds that they will suspect all our party."

On the following day William Fogo and John Mitchell wrote to Coline Campbell: "No doubt Mr Arthur will call for you ... desire you deliver him the enclosed that he may regulate himself accordingly ... be sure to press his complyance for there is absolute necessity it be followed".

On 25th August 1732 Coline Campbell agreed to buy 12 hogsheads of tobacco from Daniel McNeill "as per contract".   On 8th November Coline "met McNeil at the horse shoe and unloaded at my house" McNeill, believed to be the merchant in Macrahanish, was paid £5 for his trouble and his skipper John Mcphaden got 5 shillings. In two bills of the same date, Coline Campbell promised Daniel McNeill £181-3-10 for 16 hogsheads bought by himself and company.

(GD 1 /2 17 1-2/1)

Exports of tobacco during 1732, some to unstated destinations are given as:

Exported in the *Alexander* of Saltcoats	3 hogsheads,	2,240 lbs
" in the *Margaret* of Weems	4 "	2,856 lbs
" in the *Alexander* of		
Saltcoats to Rotterdam	14 "	9,986 lbs
" in the *Ann* of Scalaster	5 "	3,899 lbs
" in the *Ann* of Scalaster	6 "	4,794 lbs
" in the *Nancy*, Mr Glass Master	roll	1,067 lbs
" in the *Jean*		
of Irvine for Guernsey	29 "	18,687 lbs

The cargo in the *Jean* was valued at £149 - 3s 4d and we know that the voyage to Guernsey in December 32.was faked.   Other exports in this 1732 list may also have been made for the purpose of evading Customs duty.   Export figures were unreliable at that time!

Hide these Men!

William Fogo needed Coline Campbell's help to conceal two men at Inveresragan. In a second letter on 20th August he wrote: "there is a necessity of sending off two men ... pray be kind to them and give them names proper as you shall think.   Keep them as retired as possible and employ them in any work they can. All Edinburgh is scoured. I cannot tell you the event".

On 5th September, Mr Fogo wrote:
"Desire you send off these men and let them come home privately and give out that they were att the shearing ... nothing can be done with them and its better to have them home ... and lett none know where they were or who sent them ... give them twenty shillings to carry them home ... let them not see who signs it ... deliver ours to Mr Arthur and let none know he is to call att you, expect him soon ys month". The two men who had been in hiding, William Gun and Adam Anderson, duly signed on 8th September as having each received twenty shillings sterling from Coline Campbell.

By 11th September this particular crisis was resolved. Mr Fogo wrote "I wrote being then more afrightened than now. I have countermanded the former instruction and ordered them to be returned and also a new order to Mr Arthur".

The Lochetty Company Ends

The Lochetty Company was in financial difficulties. It was formally ended on 26th April 1733, but the partners continued to trade in their own names both before and after that date. From this time William Fogo's letters to Coline became distinctly unfriendly. He thought it was reasonable for Coline Campbell to pay his share of the expenses in 1732. He wrote to him on 13th April 1733 "I expect youll remitt two or three hundred pounds stg before 5th May or I will proceed to ultimate Diligence. Depend on it I am in earnest ... the next message shall be a Legal one". And on 6th May in a letter signed unusually by Henry Fogo and their partner John Mitchell "We are exceedingly pinched for money with foreign bills ... send the balances due to us ... they are long overdue". Lastly, in June, William Fogo wrote: "Its unaccountable you shoud be in advance and that I shoud be kept out of my money ... I am pinched". This letter gave the Customs duty on tobacco as 4¾d per pound.   (GD 1 / 2 17/10/3)

In October 1733 William Fogo again wrote to Coline "beg youll remitt me one hundred on my own accot and two on Compy".

Coline Campbell kept meticulous records of his expenses from 26th April 1733 to 7th May 1736. These are written in his own hand and contain information not readily available from the loose bundles of letters and accounts in the Ardchattan archives.   (GD 1 / 2 1 / 2)

A letter dated 27th July 1733 on stamped paper concludes with the statement "We hereby unanimously dissolve the Sd Compy as commencing its dissolution from 26th April last having sold to Coline Campbell the whole goods and utensils upon hand belonging to the Compy". Coline Campbell took over the stock of roll and leaf tobacco valued at £320, tobacco presses and working materials valued at £20 and shop goods valued at £230 sterling. On 20th July William Fogo, Duncan Campbell of Inverawe and John Campbell of Lossit, partners in the Lochetty Company had each agreed to pay in £132-10 in three equal instalments of £44-3-4 on 15th May 1734, at Martinmas 1734 and Martinmas 1735. William Fogo was to relieve Coline "as per Contract". The accounts of the Lochetty Company were not finalised until a meeting at Fearnoch near Taynuilt, on 29th May 1736, after many attempts to reconcile "Mitchells slate" with subsequent activities by the individual partners.

Imports of Meal –
The *Nathaniel & John* Seized at Dunstaffnage

Coline Campbell's "Waste book" lists expenses he incurred due to a "Meall Company" which he joined as partner on 8th January 1729. On the 10th of that month he met "the meallors", including Sir Duncan Campbell of Lochnell and Campbell of Achinard, at Bonawe, where "testimoney was given for his going with the copartnery".

Only three days later Coline Campbell set off on an ambitious promotional tour for the meal company. Accompanied only by a servant and two horses he went overland to Inverness, then to Elgin, Strathspey, Buchan, Banffshire, Aberdeen and Cortness, before finally awaiting replies to his letters in Edinburgh.
He was away from Inveresragan from 13th January until 12th March 1729 and claimed £25 exclusively from the meal company "for personal charges and expenses with gentlemen". Up to 16th December 1729 Coline claimed additional personal expenses of £8-13-11 "on the meall trade in this country and Lochaber" and a total of £19-8-7 on the wine and brandy trade, due from the Lochetty company.

The import of meal from Ireland into Scotland was illegal and the Admiralty Court in Inveraray has record of the seizure in July 1732 by H M Customs of the *Nathaniel & John* of Londonderry in Dunstaffnage Bay with a cargo of Irish victual.
The processes of the Court fill in the details. The petition was by Neill McNeill of Machrihanish, Riding Officer on the West Coasts against John Henderson the Master and John Davis the owner "for importing without certificate 20 bushels of malt found aboard the vessel in the harbour of Dunstaffnage". Presumably the main cargo had been unloaded before the ship was seized. When numerous local people called as witnesses could be found and induced to compear, it transpired that one of them had been put on the ship by Campbell of Achinard, who was a partner with Sir Duncan Campbell of Lochnell and Coline Campbell in the Meal Company. The Admiral Depute found the case proven (Bigwood - Admiralty Court 1732, AC 20/2/4)

There can be no doubt that the Meal Company was directly involved in this attempted import although no reference to the seizure of the *Nathaniel & John* has been seen.in the Inveresragan records.

John Davis, Merchant of Londonderry, was probably referring to the *Nathaniel & John* when he wrote to Coline Campbell on 7th August 1732: "Your letter of 1st August (with the) melancholy account of my ship being in a fair way of being condemned. I have sent Andrew McCausland to Sir Duncan (Campbell of Lochnell) and (Campbell of) Shawfield ... I expect they will yet save her from being condemned ... or will be able to buy her for a trifle. Let Andrew McCausland have what money he calls to you for".

On 4th September 1732, Mr Will Tennoch, Advocate in Edinburgh, wrote to Coline Campbell that he hoped to get Mr Davis' ship cleared. John Davis sent a number of copy letters to Coline Campbell during 1733. In one dated 20th May he mentions that his ship was stranded in January near Lochindaal and that "this goes with Mr George Stewart of Islay who is going to Bonawe or Dunstaffnage with oatmeal".

The Meal company was supplying meal to the workers at Glenkinglas Furnace, and that company became a major debtor to the Lochetty Company. William Fogo complained, in a letter to Coline Campbell dated 22nd May 1740, "as for your meal company I know nothing of it" and he refused to take responsibility for "753 bolls of meal brought into Argyle in 1733 by Campbell of Achinard, for which there is no account".

Receipts for meal sold in 1733 and 1734 were £71-17-10 and £94-13-10 respectively.

The illegal meal trade from Ireland was in full swing, much to the annoyance of Bailie John Steuart of Inverness. He had for many years legally supplied meal from the east of Scotland to his customers and kinsmen in Argyll, Skye and the north-west, including the lead-mining companies at Strontian and Glenelg. He wrote in his letter book about the seizure of the *Nathaniel and John*. "I design to go to Inverlochie next week to enquire". (Steuart Letterbook)

The *Betty* and the *Strontian* Sloop Seized at Tobermory

Coline Campbell and William Fogo also acted as merchants and suppliers to the lead mines at Strontian on Loch Sunart, where hundreds of workers and their families had to be fed.

The *Betty* of Londonderry had been chartered in July 1732 by William Kirkpatrick, merchant of Londonderry, with Joseph Kirkpatrick as Master. He was apparently replaced as Master by Daniel McLeish for this voyage. The *Betty* sailed from Derry on a Customs clearance for

Norway dated 27th July, with the following cargo:
"37 barrels and 1 tierce beef, 3 barrels of 44 lbs bacon, 1 firkin tongues, 16 casks and 16 crocks butter, 22 old cheeses and 8 new ditto, 132 bags meal, 16 boxes soap, 6 boxes candles, 35 hats, 60 pairs shoes, 150 pairs brogues & 1 hogshead Alicant wine".
On 7th August, John McNeill, Collector of Customs at Fort William, was present at Tobermory in person to seize the *Betty* and also the *Strontian* sloop, which was there by prior arrangement.

According to a "Memorial" dated 1st September "The said ship came to Tobermory in the Sound of Mull where Daniel McLeish sold his whole cargo to Mr Charles Mildmay of Strontian (who) sent a sloop to carry the cargo to the Lead mine Company stores".
The Memorial, with legal advice from Will Tennoch in Edinburgh to Daniel McLeish, states that the import of meal was against the laws of Scotland and the import of all the other items from Ireland was against the laws of Britain since 1707. He looked for ways to avoid confiscation ... suggested that the deposition by Duncan Fletcher, Master of the *Strontian* sloop could not be used by the prosecution "because it was extorted". He even suggests the defence that Duncan Fletcher was bribed using a statement dated 23rd August by John Carr, member of the crew of the *Betty* which reads:
"I John Carr of the *Betty* of Londonderry seized in Tobermory by Collector McNeil of Maryburgh, (state) that the said Collector extorted the oaths of Peter Palsey, John Cuming, James Pinkerton and myself, mariners, threatening us with imprisonment and exportation if we did not give our affidavits. And I saw Duncan Fletcher, Skipper of Mr Mildmay's sloop, with a hat and a pair of shoes out of the *Bettys* cargo so that his Disposition might be favourable to the Collector with respect to the seizure".
This statement was written by Margaret Baird and signed by John Carr.
A copy of advice by Mr Tennoch, given on 5th September is not addressed to anyone. It states: "First demand payment of the cargo from Mr Mildmay (then) Get a Summons from the Admirall of Argyle Shire against Mildmay and get a libel against him for the value of the cargo sold and delivered to him as his order".   (GD 1 / 2 9/6)

A later precept by Duncan Fletcher, mariner at Strontian, against Jerome Horsey, one of the managers of the York Building Company, was heard before the Admiralty Court in Inveraray on 7th December 1733. It reads:
"Jerome Horsey had engaged the pursuer with three men to sail the *Strontian*, the company's sloop, from 21st November 1731 to 7th August 1732, when the vessel was seized at Tobermory by John McNeill, Collector of Customs at Maryburgh, because of goods taken

on board from a brigantine lying there, McLeish master. This was by order of Charles Mildmay, then overseer of the company at Strontian".

(Bigwood AC 20/2/5)

Duncan Fletcher was claiming arrears of pay from November 1730 and "decreet was given in his favour".

It is clear that this illegal import of food for the workers at the Strontian lead mines was sanctioned at the highest level, possibly using Coline Campbell as an intermediary for John Davis of Derry.

The *Jean* of Irvine

The *Jean* was chartered by James Gray, Merchant in Irvine, in October 1732, for six months at £15 sterling per month. The Master was John Miller and he was ordered to go to Dunstaffnage where Coline Campbell of Inveresragan would give him further instructions. On 22nd October James Muirhead, a friendly merchant at Maryburgh, wrote to Coline Campbell: "I have done with the Custom House, but as for master and crew the Devil ... I cannot muster them because they have been utterly drunk since they came here. I had to hire seven hands last night to balance" (the ship). The Surveyor of Customs, Alexander Muir, was paid one pound sterling when he came to Inveresragan on 10th November.

There was trouble between John Miller and Andrew Aitken who had been engaged as Mate. On 26th November at Dunstaffnage, Aitken was paid off with thirty shillings sterling, whereupon he attacked and beat the Master "contrary to all Law and Discipline".

This complaint was signed by John Miller on 6th December at Inveresragan and witnessed by John Henderson, Master of the *Nathanial and John* of Londonderry, and by Coline Campbell of Inveresragan. The *Jean* was in the Dunstaffnage area between 20th November and 6th December and John Miller received cash of £15-11s-3d "for self and Company" from Coline Campbell as part of the Charter. Coline claimed expenses on 24th November for going to Dunstaffnage to meet the *Jean* –"to drink for workmen weighing and shipping tobacco for two days, to the freight of boats, to charges with the skipper "sundry times" and to sending an express to Fort William for a Sufferance for the export of the cargo of tobacco" – a modest total of £1 – 8s for his expenses. On 28th November "the Sheriff and others" drank five bottles of wine costing five shillings, at Coline's cellar, presumably before taking evidence about the assault on Skipper Miller.

Skipper Miller wrote a cheerful note from Appin to Coline Campbell on 8th December: "We got safe here ... would not stay longer ... We are all good friends since Aitken left". However, Coline Campbell was informed in a letter of 19th December that "the ship was stranded through the skipper and crew's drunkenness and the tobacco ashore where it was liable to damage". Coline Campbell spent eight days rectifying the situation and the expenses were considerable.

to Mr Muirhead, the merchant in Mary Burgh:

"to his trouble having entered the vessel £2-7-11 libering, shipping, weighing, coopering, watering, shipping & signing the Debenture. To the Surveyor & Land Waiter, allowance for their trouble £2- 2- 0

to sundry accounts given in by the agent £2- 0- 0

The *Jean* was at the Customs House at Fort William by 24th December, where Mr Miller paid small amounts in fees to Mr Cunningham, Comptroller of Customs and to Archibald Lang, Customs clerk. The ship sailed from Fort William on 26th December1732, cleared for Guernsey in the Channel Isles with a cargo of 29 hogsheads of leaf tobacco, which weighed 18,687 lbs.

The letters in the archives at Ardchattan Priory go some way to fill in the time gap from January to mid-May 1733. On 15th January Coline Campbell wrote to John Miller:

"You are to sail by the first fair wind to Loch Craignish and if the Captain of Craignish be at home deliver him my letter ... if not give it to his brother Alexander. If any begin to challenge your stay ... you may answer you are from Kirkudbright bound for Norway and awaiting repairs ... you may always give out your desire to sail but that your hands are ill after the fatigue of the storms. You are not to tell your cargo to any and not to open your hatches. I beg keep yourselves free of company and drink by all means lest you hazard the cargo".

On 26th March Coline sent an express to Mr Miller advising him to go to another station.

On 29th March John Miller wrote from Pennycastle of Craignish:

"The whole crew are weary having made such a long stay here. I have been furnished with necessities by the Lady Craignish but am now out of money. You have been misinformed as to my talking. If there be any Suspicions they must flow from our being here so long. I shall either continue where I am or steer to some other Creek according to Craignishs direction and advice".

By the same post Lady Craignish, signing as Helenor Smollet, wrote to Coline defending the Master: "anent Mr Miller he is very uneasy. Suspects the noise you speak of was occasioned by people who came here from Dunstaffnage in herring boats. I have known him for a fortnight together that he did not come ashore and the furthest to my house though but very seldom. As to the change house it being two miles distant you need not fear it".

On 11ᵗʰ April John Miller wrote again to Coline Campbell:
"I received from you £3 – 5s and have given Craignish a receipt. It is Craignishs opinion that we should set sail for Tobermorry and the Vessel is to pass under the name of the *John and Archibald* of Kirkudbright, John Thomson Master.
PS Please let us see you at the above place or have your orders as soon as possible for we are all weary".

On 17ᵗʰ April Coline Campbell sent an express to Mr Miller at Tobermory, and on the 3ʳᵈ May he sent another to Tobermory "to order in Mr Miller". On 17ᵗʰ May he entered the following expenses of skipper Millers freight, noting that £100 was due to Miller at £15 per month from 26ᵗʰ October 1732 to 16ᵗʰ May 1733.

"to a pilote from the horse shoe to Dunstaffnage	7s -6d
to a pilote from there to Shuna	5s -6d
to port charges at Fort William	£2 -10s -7½
to freighting and loading two boats that	
brought the tobacco from the	
back of Ardounhanish (?) to the cellar	14s
to 4 hands for one day	4s
to ditto for two days	12s"

John Blaine, a sailor aged 40, later stated that the "*Little Jean*" sailed from Irvine on 25ᵗʰ October 1732 for Dunstaffnage and Guernsey, and after loading "the ship touched at the Back of Armorgan (Ardnamurchan?) Point in the Highlands." Blaine stated that "on 11ᵗʰ May 1733 Coline Campbell of Inveresragan came on board with two boats and their crews and disloaded and carried off the cargo on board. John Miller protested (his innocence) at the mainmast against Coline Campbell of Inveresragan and James Gray of Irvine".

This was not the end of the saga. The legal processes started when James Gray asked Coline Campbell on 3ʳᵈ July 1733 to pay John Miller his due, because the owners of the *Jean* were threatening Diligence. On 13ᵗʰ September Alexander Stevenson, Writer in Edinburgh, was suing Mr Gray and Coline Campbell on behalf of John Miller for £86-15s-8d plus a penalty of £10. Five days later Coline paid Miller £78-17s-6d in full settlement.

It is fairly clear that the *Jean* did not sail to Guernsey, but "lurked" near Craignish and Tobermory until it was unloaded at sea "at the back of Armorgan" on 11ᵗʰ May and shipped back to Inveresragan,
The quantity of "export" tobacco involved was given at Fort William by Mr Lang, clerk at the Custom House in December 1732 as 29

hogsheads leaf and 6 trusses of roll, amounting to 16,776 lbs and 1,911 lbs respectively, a total of 18,687 lbs. This was "shipt on Board the *Jean* of Irvine, Master bound for Guernsey in France on account of Coline Campbell & Company". The quantity of tobacco given in a later reconciliation by the former partners of the Lochetty company was 18,675 lbs.

An undated invoice gives the amount as 23 hogsheads leaf, in numbered hogsheads, which total 15,000 lbs net, and six trusses numbered 1-6 totalling 1,911 lbs. This was stated to be shipped "on the *Jean* of Irvine, bound for Guernsey on behalf of Coline Campbell of Inveresragan & Company" and clearly refers to the same shipment.

It seems that Coline Campbell acted alone in this risky venture. William Fogo warned him on 22nd December 1732, about the risks he was taking: "The danger of relanding is three years imprisonment to the master, triple that value to the merchant – I shall have nothing to do with it. Give proper instructions to your master. Think he is not to be too heavy in his return. Can you prove the factors sales to any of your friends."

William Fogo is Arrested!
William Fogo wrote to Coline Campbell on 26th April 1733:
"Dear Coline,
No doubt youll hear of my being apprehended by a warrant on Friday last. I have applied for bail. It has put a stop to my business till I get out. My brother entered the same on Wednesday. Mr Mitchell half an hour before but because of his ordinary stupidity did not prevent this on me. Henry is (now) at Liberty. Mitchell dropt a window and escaped. I am positive to stand trial.
Your aff. Friend at present under restraint William Fogo
PS If I get out soon shall see you after the ship is discharged".

On 9th May 1733 the news was better "This day have advice that all is ended, acquittance to be granted so all former affairs are clear and I to be liberated the morrow. I am heartily weary of my quarters, would rather have your bare braes. I must swear that I sold you the tobacco contained in the certificate before the Collector and Comptroller. You should send a good quantity of leaf to your friends in the next: Let none be concerned but you, Henry and I. Mitchell is to be dismissed. He has escaped and gone for London".
The reason for the arrest of the Fogo brothers and Mr Mitchell is not known.

The Brig *Mary & Jean* and the *Agnes* Gabbart

The Lochetty Company partners were busy during 1733 with exports. Two ships were – perhaps deliberately- confused. They were the *Agnes* gabbart and the brig *Mary & Jean*.

The *Agnes* gabbart, James Beaton Master, was chartered.in January 1733. The earliest mention of this ship on 10th January 1733 refers to two of Mr Fogo's Customs certificates. One dated 10th January 1733 was for 15,000 lbs from Port Glasgow Customs, duty carried forward in Nov/Dec 1731. The other was for 6,225 lbs Greenock duty paid and served February 1732. On 7th March 1733 Mr Fogo referred to 20 hogsheads of tobacco which he had sold to Coline Campbell.

On 23rd March 1733, 48 hogsheads of leaf tobacco weighing 38,484 lbs (38,292 lbs payable) were "to be put aboard any gabert and Coline Campbell was to receive the same at the Brimilaw of Glasgow". The Broomilaw quay was used to transfer cargoes from ports in the East of Scotland, especially Alloa and Bo'ness. The same 48 hogsheads were loaded for export at Port Glasgow in the *Agnes* Gabbart. The value at 3d per lb was £478-13s and three partners of the Lochetty Company, which was still operating at that time, each incurred liability for £159-11s.

According to Mr Beaton's account of 8th June, the ship stopped at Bonawe to land miscellaneous goods for Coline Campbell and some belonging to William Somervell, younger, merchant in Renfrew.

(GD 1/2 2/2)

Mr Fogo wrote to Coline on 2nd July: "The gabert sailed (from Port Glasgow) on 23rd June with 48 hhds. "Coline Campbell records on 29th June 1733 "48 hogsheads tobacco discharged at the cellar from the *Agnes* Gabbart. Required 8 hands for 2 days Libering the Gabbart".

Coline's expenses for 17th July were on account of "4 hands to ship hogsheads to freight and bringing home wine etc bought of Mr John Somervell".

This shipment was clearly a relanding of duty-free tobacco.

In July 1733 the *Mary and Jean* of Gourock, a brigantine of 40 tons burden, was also chartered by William Fogo and Archibald Campbell, Merchant in Glasgow – possibly the future Manager at Oban. The Master was Jeremiah Campbell (or John McNeil). Mr Fogo wrote to Coline Campbell: "Mr Campbell has freighted the brig at £10-10s per month for three months – you to pay mens wages and victualling, the same terms as Arthur, there being no other to be got. Have ready what route you propose and leaf tobacco to be weighed and pressed". On 6th August Mr Fogo wrote: "Hope the brig is now sailed" and on 4th September: "Mitchell is making a great noise in Glasgow about his not being paid and has told several your business, a good many lies,

38

particularly that you employed him to liber some goods and that you desired him to ship them". John Mitchell, a partner or associate in Mr Fogo's office, had been dismissed after the brothers had been arrested in May.

Coline Campbell's expenses include the following entries at this time. 4th August 1733: "to Libering 62 hhds and 8 Turses (45,702 lbs) at Fort William from the *Mary & Jean*.
A later account by the partners states that 38,484 lbs of tobacco were dispatched in the *Mary & Jean* for Campvire in Holland on 2nd August 1733. This was exactly the same amount as the 48 hogsheads delivered to Inveresragan from the *Agnes* on 29th June. Coline Campbell's expenses were:

"To vessels clearance and to Mr Lang (Customs Clerk) for his
trouble extraordinary   £1
To charges at Ft Wm, with servant and 2 horses, 10 days
                                         £8 – 8s - 10d.

Cash paid to John McNeil,
master of *Mary & Jean*, wages   £4
22nd August: bringing tobacco from Bonaw,
cash James Beaton   £2 "

(This last receipt was dated 4th July and refers to the *Agnes* Gabbart).
12th November: "to a boat and 4 hands when the *Mary & Jean* arrived."
21st November: "to freight with boat and 4 hands going to Kerola (Kerrera) & return, after sending off the vessel". (Apparently in the nick of time!) .

22 November: "the Collector of Fort William having come in order to search for the tobacco, on Information.

to Extraordinary Charges on the occasion   £21
dram and meal to 12 men
and charges at Bunaw   £2 - 6s
to incidents at Connel for a night &
2 days with the Collr & others that
came to Divert him   £1–12– 8½
to freight of a boat & hands to bring me home   2 – 6d"

It is clear that the *Mary & Jean* returned in November 1733 to reland at Horseshoe Bay on Kerrera most of the tobacco shipped in August, and that it barely escaped capture.

Fort William Customs had information that the *Mary & Jean* relanded some tobacco near Cork in Ireland, on its way to Campvire in Holland.

An undated account at Inveresragan confirms that the amounts of tobacco sold in Ireland as well as in Guernsey on this voyage were quite small, as follows: (GD1 / 2 17 2/2)

"Tobacco sold from the *Mary & Jean* of Gourock
Sold upon the Coast of Ireland to:
Dennis Calachan 3 hhds 2247 lbs at 3¾d

	paid cash	£15
	by bill	£19-13- 8
	total	£34-13- 8
Silvester Dee	2 hhds 1477 lbs at 3¾d	
	by cash	£11-10
	by bill	£11-11- 4
	total	£23- 1- 4

William Bishop 2 hhds 1712 lbs

	by cash	£12
	By bill	£14-15
	Total	£26-15
	Total bills	£45-19- 3

lying in John Forrest's hands. Now in Cork

Sold in Guernsey
sold Nicolas larson 20 cwts: 0 qtrs: 5 lbs at 24s per cwt £24- 0- 5
sold Joseph measner 432 lbs at 21 per cwt £ 4-10- 9
637 lbs at 25 per cwt £ 7-19- 3
2 cut hhds £ 2-10
3 cut hhds, 1304 lb at 17 per. £11- 1- 6
total £26- 1- 6".

The above sales represent about 16 hogsheads, which tallies with a later reconciliation of tobacco stocks and sales from Inveresragan. This states that 31,036 lbs of leaf in 46 numbered hogsheads and 8 trusses of roll weighing 2525 lbs were "returned from Guernsey". This was another relanding free of Customs duty.
The confusion between the two ships, the *Agnes* Gabbart and the brigantine *Mary & Jean* is outlined in an undated memo of 1734 written, third person, in Coline Campbell's own hand.

"For several years past he manufactured leaf tobacco into rolls for country and for foreign parts. He built several Cellars wherein he also prepared several other goods. On 2nd August last (1733) he exported 45,000 lbs leaf and roll by the *Mary & Jean* of Gourock. The debenture was refused because the ship was the *Agnes* Gabbart of Glasgow and some of the tobacco was relanded about Cork in Ireland. Jeremiah Campbell, Master of the *Mary & Jean*, carried 60 hogsheads leaf, 8 trusses roll and 2 casks of cut tobacco. It is denied that any part of this was relanded. Some malicious person Informed that the

whole quantity was relanded and brought to my Cellars".
On 3rd January 1734 Coline Campbell claimed expenses "while viewing the Concerns at Dunstaffnage & Oban".
This may well be the first indication that Oban was to play a part in tobacco smuggling.

Deliveries to Fort William of 22,000 lbs from the *Diamond's* 1732 cargo, less 7000 lbs which were exported from there, left a balance of 15,000 lbs of leaf tobacco. Mr Fogo wrote to Coline on 14th January 1734: "You know that I sold you 20 odd thousand ex-Diamond. You can swear you bought it in a fair way from me". A certificate refers to 48 hogsheads in the *Mary and Jean* of Gourock but this was also the amount of leaf tobacco shipped on the *Agnes* Gabbart. These certificates and debentures were the cause of confusion to the participants at the time. What hope have we to disentangle them today!

Tobacco Seized at Inveresragan
On 20th and 21st March 1734 Coline Campbell wrote to Mr Fogo: "Alexander Muir, Surveyor at Fort William, came with a party and seized all the tobacco in my cellars 24,000 lbs before this was Embezeled. The Surveyor broke open the cellars and took everything away without weighing it".

William Fogo wasted no time in giving advice on how to recover from the losses sustained at Inveresragan. The very day after the seizure in March – and how did he hear so quickly - he wrote to Coline "Go to Ft Wm and give Mr Muir (the Surveyor) a bill of sale for the tobacco seized at 10 pence per pound. Swear an affidavit before a J P and then go to Edinburgh and protest. They'll never prove it was relanded. If they refused to weigh it at your Cellar they must weigh it at Ft Wm, then youll know the quantity then add 2000 for Embezlements, or more as you think proper. Also mention that part of it is the remains of a certificate ex-*Diamond* 1732 - that it was sold in Guernsey. They must prove it never was landed on foreign ground or exported".
Coline later gave the total seized as 22,975 lbs and estimated ihe loss between seizure and weighing at the Custom House of 7,025 lbs. He asacribed this to "Imbeselments, pilferages and other damage between seizure and weighing". Priced at tenpence per pound for local sale the total value was £1,249-12-8 and the tobacco "lost in transit" was valued at £292-8-10.

The background to this event is contained in a statement made by the informer Hugh Campbell, a snuff-maker at Bonawe, on 31st May 1734. "That in february was put on board one McNeills vessel 60 hogsheads at Inveresragan which was carried to Fort wm & there weighed. That the said vessel came upon the coast with tobacco and ran the same at Dunstafnage – the tobacco was from there brought in open boats to the cellars of Coline Campbell at Inveresragan – the same as was afterwards seized in March. That Alexander Clemie tobacco spinner was employed in the shipping outwards as well as Running in this tobacco".

A legal Petition to Collector McNeill on Coline Campbell's behalf, states. "Being a manufacturer of tobacco he lately had about 30,000 libs weight some in hhds others part leaf and roll ... siezed ... a good deal being lost and Imbezeld in this carrying off". Furthermore not all the tobacco seized had been brought by sea but that quite a lot had come by land.

That the informer Hugh Campbell had made malicious charges because he owed money and Coline Campbell had demanded repayment "with some sharpness threatening rigour and severity if he did not". The Petition concludes with the hopeful statement that "the Laws which make a mans goods his property when in his possession not Directly coming from the water syde or when they have been a month in his possession are Deemed as if the Duties had been paid".

On 21st September 1734 Collector McNeill personally took sworn evidence at Inveresragan from Archibald Gillies, schoolteacher at Ardchattan, George Stevenson, shopkeeper at Inveresragan, Alexander Clemie, tobacco spinner there, Donald McFarlane, "commonly called McAndra", boatman at Bunaw and two indwellers there. None of them had seen or heard anything about the "running and relanding of tobacco at Inveresragan. The last three had certainly not assisted in loading or transporting tobacco "on McNeill's Vessell ... except that 7 or 8 months ago they assisted in bringing a small quantity of leaf and roll tobacco in Company of George Stevenson, from oban to Inveresragan cellars and that they heard it was sold a Customer who broke his bargain and therefore it was brought back".
.

The problem of restocking the empty cellars had been quickly solved. On 20th April, only a month after the seizure, William Fogo wrote to Coline Campbell: "All the things you ordered with 32 hogsheads tobacco are in the gabert. The workmen will be with Clemie and the cooper". He went on: "Send 6 of the best to a cellar in Bonawe: the rest to your cellar if good for spinning. My advice to you is to sell the tobacco to some friend and take his bill for it and cause him ship it off in his name. So let this be done as soon as the gabert arrives. I think your brother or Inveraws brother may do it".

On 20th April 1734 a second letter from William Fogo to Coline

Campbell reads: "Delivered your paper to Mr Stewart, attorney at Edinburgh who gave in a petition to the Commissioners, Wasbie, Sir James Campbell and Drummond being at the Board. As to the tobacco taken away, they'll attempt to prove relanding but it will be difficult. Lord Islay and Sir James will support you. Am told it's a Campbell that informed and some laff and say its Campbell against Campbell. To provoke his revenge you had better paid him ten times his account as to be put to this charge. There is no help for it now but take care who you employ.
It would help if he retracted his accusation".

On 15th May 1734 Mr Fogo wrote: "To disappoint those Gentlemen of prejudice against you think that fellow's recantation is a good step. If you give him anything see it be offered by some other hand and delayed until the event".

Coline Campbell was in Edinburgh attempting to influence people in his favour from 8th May to 10th July 1734. Among others he saw Lord Cathcart and reminded him that £160 was owed by the Glenkinglas company to the former Lochetty partners.

Coline Campbell's efforts met with success. Mr Fogo wrote to him on 6th July 1734: "Go to Ft Wm and demand to recover your tobacco and transport it to your warehouse. You are to demand your certificate for 20,000 ex *Diamond* from the Collector. I shall send you a copy if they cannot do it off the print certificate".
The cost of recovering the seized tobacco was heavy. Coline Campbell claimed:
"8th May to 8th July to Charges going to Edr with horses & servtt attending the

Custom house of Exchequer	£34-16s- 6d
for recovering the tobacco seized from the cellars	
cash to Mr Ramsay for advice	£ 5
to Collr McNeill at Edr	£ 2- 2s
cash paid to James Stuart	£10-16s- 6d
Sundry necessarys viz Body Cloathes	
bought by Coline at Edr that otherwise	
he had no occasion for	£22-15s- 7d"

To these expenses were added the cost of bringing the seized tobacco back to the cellars at Inveresragan, namely:

12th July to charges at Ft wm recovering	
the tobacco	£ 3-13s- 3½d
Libering (£1-2s) couper (2s) wages	
& drink (19s) etc	£ 3- 10s- 6d
To freight of the vessel	£10"

The *Glasgow Packet* of Greenock

The 1734 voyage to Rotterdam by the *Glasgow Packet* of Greenock, Robert Sinclair Master, can be covered in some detail.

(GD1/2 1/2 1/3).

The vessel arrived at Bonawe on 30th August and by 5th September it was loaded with 34 hogsheads of tobacco for export, to be consigned to Alexander Naughten, a tailor in Rotterdam. Equal Copartners in the voyage were William and Henry Fogo and Coline Campbell of Inveresragan. The tobacco was unloaded at Fort William and on 13th September reloaded there as 32 numbered hogsheads weighing 25,498 lbs of leaf (later 25,554 lbs or 228 cwts 0 qtrs 18 lbs) and 2,578 lbs in 169 rolls, to be put into two hogsheads. The ship sailed for Rotterdam on 16th September and returned to the Sound of Mull and Kerrera on 28th November.

The expenses incurred by Coline Campbell for the outward voyage were:

"Going to Fort William to arrange export	£ 6-12 - 6d
Entry inwards	12 - 6d
Entry outwards for parts abroad	£ 1- 5
Weigher, cooper, packmen, watchers, cheese. butter	£ 2- 7 - 6d
Three 5 year old bullocks & 1 cow for the Ship	£ 5- 0
Allowance of 2 hhds, 1200 lbs to Comptr & Svr	£ 6- 3
To cash for the Skipper	£ 2-12 - 6d
To 10 pints of brandy for the Master	£ 1- 3 - 4d
To cash paid the landwaiter on the vessel till she cleared the District	£ 2-2"

(GD 1/ 2 1/ 2)

Other charges were noted on 21st September as:

"Charges with the Collector & Comptroller	£ 1- 5
to the Tidewaiter	£ 2- 2
to extraordinary charges	£12 - 0"

Elsewhere it was noted that the Customs Surveyor, Mr Muir, had been paid £0-10-6 on the journey to Fort William, and that the bill for cooperage of 36 hogsheads was £1-5-9.

The allowance of 2 hhds, above, account for the reduction from 36 to 34 in the quantity for export: The £12 for "extraordinary charges" could be a bribe or fee.

On 13th September Collector John McNeill and Comptroller John Comrie at Fort William signed that all duties had been paid and secured inward at Port Glasgow by Wm & Henry Fogo and by John Blair. The certificate was dated 8th April 1734. All this was legal.

A detailed "Accompt of Sale and Nate Proceeds" of the sale of 28 hogsheads of tobacco by Alexander Naughten, Merchant in Rotterdam

and consigned by the *Glasgow Packet*, Robert Sinclare Master", netted Coline Campbell and the Fogo brothers a useful £368- 14- 4 each, after all expenses.   (Illustrated p. 46)
The release of Customs Duty on the exported tobacco, totalling 25,498 lbs, amounted to:

The old Subsidy	£ 79	- 11	- 1½ d
The new Subsidy	£ 90	- 4	- 4¾ d
One-third Subsidy	£ 30	- 1	- 5½ d
Additional Duty	£ 90	- 4	- 4¾ d
Impost on tobacco	£270	- 13	- 2¼ d
Total	£560	- 14	- 6¾ d

John Comrie, the new Comptroller at Fort William gave this good news in a friendly letter to Coline Campbell dated 19th October 1734. (the former Comptroller Adam Cunningham became a merchant in Maryburgh). The letter reads:
"Dear Colin
(The delay) occasioned by Muirs not Certifying till I got him this Day with some difficulty, seeing you know he cares little to come near the Custom House.
I have enclosed your Debentures duely Exped(ited) along with John Somervell who promises to deliver this letter.
I am, Dear Sir, Your most P. obliged humble Ser   John Comrie".
                                        (GD 1/ 2 9/8)

On 11th November, Mr Fogo wrote of the *Glasgow Packet* which was returning from Holland: "So look out for them and have everything prepared against they touch. Dispatch the ship in to Clyde in her ballast and without loss of time carried into your country. Pray take care of the 4 trunks marked W F for they are valuable and not bulky so that you can soon order them down or lodge them safely till they be sent for. Intreat youll be cautious and keep all quiet, seeing the ship is not to come in or stop in your coast. Think it can make no noise if right gone about. All must depend on your prudence".
Dutch goods loaded at Rotterdam for Coline Campbell and William & Henry Fogo on 22nd October for the return voyage were priced at a massive total of £1,964 -10 -8d.
The imported shop goods are too numerous to be listed in detail.
                                        (GD 1 / 2 and 1 / 3)
The major items which were landed at Kerrera on 28th November before the ship reached Clyde Customs were:

500 lbs gunpowder (for the Strontian lead mines)	£125
12 barrels of soap	£240
2 casks of whalebeards (50 and 100 lbs)	£250
allom, rock indigo, madder (in casks)	£227
bohea, Imperial & green tea	£257

Accompt of Sale & Nate Proceeds of Hogsheads Tobacco Sold by Alexander Naughten for Account of Messr William & Henry Fogo & Colin Campbell each's in Company, Consigned me by the Glasgow Packet, Robert Sinclare Master as under Viz:

N°16. 626.70	N°12. 636.70	N°7. 654.180
26. 628.80	9. 622.110	25. 628. 30
13. 636.66	18. 640.80	8. 672. 90
1.596.100	1. 654. 60	23. 662. 70
10. 580.70	11. 662.66	17. 542.90
19. 606. 60	15. 666. 76	14. 530. 46
27. 670.36	30. 586. 86	20. 638. 30
41. 722.110	3. 656. 66	22. 660. 70
2. 512. 86	5. 620. 80	6. 636. 100
28. 590. 46	9 hhds 5742. 694	9 hhds 5622. 706

CC

10 hhds 6166. 724
9 hhds 5742. 694
9 hhds 5622. 706

In all 28 hhds 17530.2124

Off - 2124 ℔ for Refraction
15406
Off - 1232 ℔ for 8 per Cent.
In all 14174 ℔ payable leaf Tobacco - at 2⅜ pr ℔ /1653.3 .
Off 2 pr Cent - /.33.13" /1619.10..
3 Hogsheads Leaf Tobacco Viz: N°21. 29 & 31 Sold over head for - - /.37.. ..
3 Hogsheads Roll Tobacco Viz: N°13. 14 & 15 Sold over head for - /.60.. .. ..
/1716.10 ..

Deduce Charges as under. Viz:
Entry Passport & Surveyors - - - - /61.4..
Johns Excise - - - - /85.. ..
Lighterage & Landing - - - - /13.12..
Staying to Warehouse - - - - /13.12..
Paid Robert Sinclare pr Receipt £31.3.. Ster. at /11.4. p 14 /348.17.8
Rolling in & out - - - - /.5..2..
Cooperring & Nails - - - - /.17.. ..
One half Weighouse dues - - - - /.32..6..
One half Brokerage - - - - /.17.. ..
One half Refraction Masters Fees - - - /.8.10..
Warehouse Rent & Spent at Sale - - - /.3.4..
Commission - - at 2 pr Cent /.35.. .. /640.14.8
Nate Proceeds - - - /1106.2.8

Mr William Fogo's ⅓ Nate Proceeds being /368.14.2
Mr Henry Fogo's ⅓ Nate Proceeds being /368.14.2
Mr Colin Campbell's ⅓ Nate Proceeds being /368.14.2 /1106.2.8
Rotterdam 9 Octr 1734 Errors Excepted
Alexr Naughten

An account of a profitable voyage in 1734 to Campvire in Holland, by the Glasgow Packet of Greenock. The sale of 28 hogsheads of leaf tobacco yielded each of the partners a profit of £368 Sterling. In addition six unsold hogsheads were relanded duty-free at Inveresragan when the ship returned with "Dutch Goods".
© Ardchattan Priory Archives.

½ hogshead arrack (45 stoups) at £3-10s   £159
Javan coffee beards at 18s per bag
1 hamper of 48 bottles burgundy wine
4 ankers ginever, 20 gross corks
17 reams of cardous paper at £5   £ 85
  glass & chinaware, chamber pots, lace, cambrick etc

Tucked away in the priced list of imports was the unpriced item "6 hogsheads leaf tobacco". Clearly this accounted for the discrepancy between 34 hogsheads shipped and 28 listed as sold by Mr Naughten. The 6 hogsheads were certainly relanded where they started from – in Coline Campbell's cellars, to be sold later and duty-free.
Coline listed one other item "in compliment":
24 bottles burgundy and 26 bottles of arrack: to Sir James Campbell of Achnabreck.
This was undoubtedly a "thank you" for help given in recovering the tobacco.seized in March 1734.
Coline claimed the following expenses on 28th November
"when the *Glasgow Packet* returned to Sound of Mull, charges going to Kerola:
2 coaster boats & 12 hands to bring up the goods   £2
discharging the boats & Cellaring the goods   £0-6- 8"

Two further opportunities to reland tobacco were noted in 1734.
On 11th October, Mr Fogo wrote "Order the enclosed to be delivered Mr Arthur if he calls at horse shoe. We considered Fort William but we are insured only for the east coast. If you see him you may get any thing they can spare". Captain Robert Arthur was on his way back from Virginia in the *Diamond* to Alloa Custom House on the East Coast.
On 19th October Mr Fogo wrote: "Mr Bailie of Morton's brother Alexander has 13 hogsheads tobacco – suggest 5d per pound delivered your warehouse payable in 6 and 12 months, if you find him sufficient security with some person of good command here".

On 16th November Mr Fogo rebuked Coline Campbell: "Youll never learn. The oath you was to swear was that the quantity of 25,498 pounds tobacco (was) shipped on board the *Glasgow Packet* of Greenock, Robert Sinclair Master, for Rotterdam. You must go directly to Fort William. They must write a new one because it cannot be mended. It must be the same date".
And on 18th November "You should have paid your third of the 48 hogsheads long ago. Send the good to England or London in place of the 23, which must be exported. Our ship is gone north: all leaf threepence farthing if not more".

Coline was again in Edinburgh "on company business, abroad above a month with servtt and 2 horses". On 10th December 1734 he charged the Oban company £17-18-6 expenses and for £1-16-10 paid to James Stuart.

The *Black Bitch* Affair: Tobacco Seized at Airth

The *Black Bitch* of Elphinstone, William Hodge Master, was owned by John Hyndman. The vessel was first employed on a four-month charter drawn up on 15th March 1735 at Airth, near Alloa on the Forth Estuary. On 8th April she was loaded at Airth with 43 hogsheads of leaf tobacco weighing 31,760 pounds. This was part of the *Diamond*'s January 1735 cargo of 100 hogsheads or 60,000 pounds, out of a total of 297 hogsheads, which had been bonded at Alloa Custom House on 2nd January 1735 by Coline Campbell and by William and Henry Fogo. The Duty was £2,666-13s-4d Sterling half of which was due for payment before 8th July 1735. (See Oban Company and Captain Robert Arthur, below)

The partners' stated intention was to export 28 hogsheads of tobacco to Campvire in Holland and to store 15 hogsheads at Inveresragan for inland consumption. A detailed bill of loading gives the number, weight and quality of every hogshead and is headed "from Airth to Coline Campbell and Company at Inveresragan per Fort William".

(Illustrated pp. 50, 51)

The ship set sail from Airth for Fort William on 15th April 1735.

William Fogo's three-page letter to Coline Campbell dated 23rd April 1735 spells out an intended deception. "The ship sailed eight days ago with a fair wind. They have orders to advise you from the horse shoe I have marked 15 hhds amounting to 11,532 lbs which you are to keep and the rest to be sent Coastways viz 28 hhds amounting to 20,228 lbs which you are to ship for London and consign to Messrs Robert and William Freads. You must go to Fort William when she comes there and get a sufferance to unload at your cellar and get a certificate to cancel the coast bond and get a sufferance to ship aboard 28 hhds which must be taken to Fort William and they may weigh one of ten and give you a coast clearance to London. You are to put the 28 hhds into your warehouse by themselves and alter their numbers from 1-28 but in your invoice you keep the old numbers on one column and the new on another and the weight. Then draw out a clean invoice to give to the Custom house with the new numbers only. The number 3 hhd of roll, could not get into the entry in the hatch way so (you) must get it out as not concerned when it come to your cellar. The folks at Fort William need know nothing of it. Pray make all dispatch ... much depends on getting your design finished and the ship dispatched. Hope you have ink: If not erase out the numbers with the scraper but let none see it done: one with yourself that you can trust. Also scrape out all marks that may be on the casks, or numbers, or markings made in Virginia. You need not detain the ship at your warehouse above a day. Let not the crew know anything but its tobacco out of your cellars that was there. You must clear out from Fort William and be as sparing as possible and at the same time humour them".

There was a hitch in the signing by Collector John McNeill at Fort William.

On 5th May William Fogo wrote to Coline Campbell: " I see noe reason for the Collr refusing ... its what he has thought of since I parted with him, you must certainly prevail with him and tell him that I am to see him in June and shall take a botle with you and him and thankfully reward all his civilities att same time pay him his fees ... pretty Large let none of the rest know it & not let him know what you gave ye Comp(trolle)r or Surveyor." This approach was apparently successful. The sufferance reads:

"Port: Fort William
Suffer Colin Campbell to carry to Fort William twenty thousand weight leaff tobaco returned him by a write of delivery from the Exchqwer on Board the *Black Bich* of Elphistoun given at Fort William this 12th May 1735
(signed) John McNeill Collector".

The reason for renumbering the hogsheads is not known but the *Black Bitch* sailed from Fort William for London with 28 hogsheads of tobacco, consigned to Messrs Robert and William Freads, on 23rd May 1735.

Coline Campbells expenses were:

11th May: to workmen and coopers Shoaring tobacco and shipping again. Wages of hands loading and unloading at my house and cellaring: £   1 - 6s
21st May: to charges at Ft wm to clear out the vessel for London with 28 hhds.
to workmen & coopers at Ft wm   £   4 - 10s
to the waiter who came to see the Tobacco loaded   £   2
to the skipper per receipt   £ 12 - 7s

Captain Hodge left London on 14th July and arrived back at Airth on the 26th July. On that day Mr Fogo wrote "would send her straight to Holland and from that with Lintseed to the firth which will end our voyage".

There is an account dated 24th June 1735, which must refer to the disposal of the same 28 hogsheads. It reads as follows:

"To sundry charges, 28 hogsheads
Ex Fort William   £ 31 - 8 - 6d
Cash paid the captain   £ 16 - 17 - 6d
Sundry charges at delivery   £ 22 - 19 - 8
Net proceeds carried to your account current   £477 -   1s

Invoyce of 44 hhds pr Black Bitch
1735   William Hodge mastr from Airth To
mark   Coline Campbell & Compy att
CC   Inveresegan pr Fort william

No + 331 " 6 " 2 " 20 good Repaile
    × 204 " 6 " 1 " 10 Ditto
    + 246 " 7 " 1 " 21 Ditto
    £ 201 " 5 " 2 " 13 --- 2nd: good
    £ 327 " 6 " 2 " 14 -- good no 1
    £ 281 " 5 " 0 " 18 -- good no 1 Boll: Large
    £ 296 " 7 " 2 " 11 -- pretty good no 2
10 £ 244 " 7 " 1 " 00 -- good well smelled no 1 Large —
    £ 213 " 6 " 3 " 11 — 2/3 stow good no 1 —
    × 220 " 7 " 2 " 18 -- good well smelled no 1
         _____
         67 " 0 " 24

    × 249 --- 6 " 3 " 11 --- well smelled no 1 —
    × 3 " 5 " 2 " 25 — 2nd ifferant gd —
    £ 168 " 6 " 1 " 25 — Large Bright well smelled no 1 —
    £ 166 " 6 " 0 " 26 -- pretty good no 2 —
    £ 151 " 6 " 2 " 14 -- 2nd iff good no 2
    £ 195 " 6 " 3 " 03 -- good well smelled no 1 one Cake Luggs
10 + 165 " 8 " 2 " 00 -- good well smelled no 1
    £ 175 " 7 " 0 " 21 -- pretty good no 2 Bulge & Boll: Best
    × 172 " 6 " 1 " 17 -- good well smelled no 1 —
    + 163 " 8 " 0 " 14 -- good no 1 Bulge & Boll: 3 sy 1.
         _____
         68 " 3 " 15

    £ 179 " 7 " 0 " 21 -- good no 1 wt some Luggs —
    £ 184 " 6 " 2 " 23 -- well smelled 2nd iff: good no 1
10 × 193 " 7 " 0 " 14 -- good no 1 well smelled
    × 197 " 6 " 3 " 22 --- Ditto —
    £ 170 " 7 " 0 " 11 -- Ditto wt small cake stem —
    £ 188 " 5 " 1 " 00 -- 2nd iff good no 1
    £ 8 " 5 " 0 " 8 -- 2nd ifferent good —
    £ 38 " 6 " 2 " 19 -- 2nd iff good no 1
    + 4 " 5 " 2 " 16 -- 2nd ifferent —
    × 120 " 6 " 2 " 27 -- good no 1 top & Boll: Best —
         _____
         65 " 1 " 21

Detailed "bill of loading" for the Black Bitch sailing from Airth, near Alloa to Fort William
Customs House. It was intended to renumber fifteen hogsheads of tobacco from this cargo
secretly at Inveresragan. © Ardchattan Priory Archives.

50

£ 109 " 6 " 3 " 6 Indiff good no2
£ 118 " 6 " 2 " 21 ... good no2 Boll best —
2/ 19 " 6 " 2 " 18 ... good no2 Large
£ 113 " 6 " 0 " 14 ~ Large & bright good no2
£ 125 " 6 " 1 " 21 Indiff good no1 alittle cutt
× 44 " 6 " 2 " 5 ~ good no1
£ 112 " 6 " 0 " 0 " Indiff good
£ 12 " 5 " 1 " 11 pretty good no2 Boll: best —
+ 55 " 6 " 1 " 00 ... good no1 light
£ 122 " 6 " 1 " 23 ~ good no1 Cake in Boll: worse
                    ─────────────
                    63 " 1 " 7

2/+ 39 " 6 " 1 " 9 ~ Indiff good no1 top best —
 102 " 6 " 3 " 16 ~ Indiff good no2 —
× 68 " 5 " 2 " 00 Indiff good —
 × 3 " 5 " 2 " 25 roll — — Returned —
                    ─────────────
                    24 " 1 " 22

Osd of no 3 roll ... 5 " 2 " 29
        leaf 18 " 2 " 25 - - - - - - - - - -   18 " 2 " 25
                                                       63 " 1 " 7
                                                       65 " 1 " 21
                                                       68 " 3 " 15
                                                       67 " 0 " 24
                                                       ─────────────
                                                       283 " 2 " 8
                                                       283   56
                                                       283   64
                                                       28364
Deduct 4 @ p Hh —43.hh:. ... 31760 — exeport —
                                              172
                                        31588 @ 3 £394 " 17:0
To 26 Boll meal at 6 @ £13 — ~
To 43 oll learn at 5½ ... 19.8½
To home & cariage of learn ... 7
To making bags 13 cariage 7 ... 1.8   £14 " 2 " 7½
To workmen tramping ... 8
To Charges shipping &c ... ps. ...   2 . 2 . 6
To Cash given Hodge master to acct ...   10.0
To charges of charter party & freight: ... 3 " 1 " 6
      ing &c ...   ────────────
To Coals acct not yet gott in ...   £17 . 16 . 7½

Contras
11 July by Hugh Sutherland, 6 hhds, 4178 lbs nett £122 - 17 - 6d
17 July by Thos Walker, 8 hhds, 5551 lbs nett   £164 - 7 - 6d
29 July by Archibald Astley 14 hhds, 9249 lbs nett £261 - 1 - 8d
total 28 hhds   £548 - 6 -8d"

These deliveries may have been to customers of Messrs Freads in London.
The stated nett profit on this voyage was only about £70, but additional profit may have been made from the hogsheads which were renumbered and substituted at Inveresragan.

On 25th August Captain Hodge set sail from Airth with 12 hogsheads of leaf tobacco – 9,254 lbs – consigned to George and David Gregory in Rotterdam. He left Campvire in Holland on 8th October and returned to Airth with "Dutch goods" on 30th October, before setting off for Fort William again with tobacco which was unloaded at Dunstaffnage.

Coline Campbell records "going to Dunstaffnage to meet Mr Hodge" on 6th December. On 13th December he notes his: expenses:
"to boats hands shoaring tob from the ships   £ 1 -   4 - 6
to incidents with the Campbell crew   19 - 6"

On 23rd December he notes:
"Cash to Mr Hodge per receipt   £19
to small charges at Maryburgh & Dunstaffnage £ 5 -   5
to Collr (£6-6), to Comptr (£6-6), tidewaiter (£2-2) £14 - 14
to Surveyor and landwaiter   10 - 10
own charges 13th Dec. to 1st January 1736
with Customs   £ 9 - 18 - 5"
On 24th December Captain Hodge submitted an invoice to Coline Campbell for four months pay at £15 per month from August to 15th December and some incidentals.
At least 2,000 lbs of cut and rolled tobacco were brought to Inveresragan from Airth on this voyage.

There are interesting details of pilotage on this 1735 voyage from Campvire round the north of Scotland to Fort William as follows:
"by October 15th Pilotage from Campvire   - 18s 4d
Pilotage into wisura, orkney   - 7s 6d
into Stromness   5s
to Lochaber   £ 4 - 10s
December 9th Pilot castle Duart to Dunstaffnage   6s 2d
December 14th Pilot from the Connell   1s
Total   £ 6 - 8s"

Captain Hodge left Fort William on 5th February 1736, having loaded 29 hogsheads of roll tobacco weighing 23,305 lbs. He was ostensibly bound for Campvire in Holland. The *Black Bitch* reached Airth on 29th February where she was boarded by the Customs from Alloa and her cargo of tobacco seized.

A Customs memo dated 9th August 1736 states that the ship came into Airth loaded six or seven weeks after it cleared from Fort William for Campvire in Holland. The officers at Alloa boarded her and the Master produced the clearance "got at Fort William which, not answering to the weight of hhds on board, the tobacco was seized and since Condemned without any persons claiming the same". The Customs memo went on to give Coline Campbell's explanation that the tobacco wasn't his but seemed to be "tobacco imported by the skipper on his own behalf making use of Mr Campbell's clearance from Fort William which he needed not to give up in Holland for that purpose".

A later reconciliation by the Oban partners gave the amount of tobacco seized at Airth as 28,050 lbs, not the 29 hogsheads of 23,305 lbs loaded at Fort William Custom House. Extra tobacco may have been loaded at Inveresragan or Oban after the ship sailed from Fort William. On 19th June the partners calculated the loss as 48 hogsheads at £494-2-0 which was £164-14-0 each due from William Fogo, Henry Fogo and Coline Campbell.

This loss came on top of the final reckoning from the ending of the Lochetty Company in 1733. This final calculation, agreed on 29th May 1736, gave the Lochetty Company debts as £588-15-2½, to be met equally by the same three partners.

. Why the ship touched at Airth is not clear but John Ogilvie, a merchant at Airth, had an interest in the cargo.

John Ogilvie sometimes concealed his own tobacco at Inveresragan. For example on 5th July 1736, William Fogo wrote to Coline: "ogilvie (has) purchased 25 qtys of meal" (i.e. tobacco),"which may be with you next month. You shoud empty your warehouse and land it there and let her fall down to Dunstaffnage and then you send for a sufferance to ship 25 and some more ... and all on the Credite of the Diamond 1735/36 and hope that by that time youll have as much down as will augur that qty att least".

When the *Black Bitch* was seized its cargo included a bar of lead (from Strontian) which weighed 1 ton 11¼ cwts. On 26th March 1736 Coline Campbell noted this lead to be "in the hands of John Ogilvy at Airth, ex *Black Bitch*". Perhaps Mr Ogilvie took the lead as part compensation for his losses.

William Fogo had fallen out with Coline Campbell over the seizure. John Cowan, the principal merchant in Stirling, was also involved in the affair of the *Black Bitch*.   Back from a visit to Stirling, William Fogo wrote to Coline Campbell on 17th April 1736:

"Its pretty odd you shoud offer Cowan a bill on me ... did I order any of those effects from him: wish you woud think how to pay before you take on ... I can do you litle service tho most readie

as to my using your name does it not appear to every man you were the exporter ... do I not averr your tob: was sold in Holld and that it is not yours what woud you have me say to join you in such a stupid action that I know nothing of ... your insinuations woud provoake any man when I have done so much for you ... I wrote you it was owing to Collonsa and Young so litle can you say I forced you into that concern (the Oban company) ... wish you woud do things amicably ... if you incline to be out of that concern ... perhaps Young will take yours also if you apply".

The problems caused by "the cursed bitch", rumbled on during 1736, with legal consultations in April. "Its odd you coud not of all subjects clear off Hodge till he sailed from fort william" wrote Mr Fogo to Coline Campbell on 1st April. On the 14th April he and his brother signed a letter to Coline from Stirling. "I can inform nothing further about Hodge ... you are to tell Capt Campbell that your tob: was exported and that you have nothing to do with that taken on the coast and that all you want is that they may allow you your tob: without a prosecution ... and that the tob: seized is not that which was shypt for exportation then found in same shype on her return from forrain parts.

Beg your outmost endeavours to raise money and remitt wtout loss of time ... we have a great many demands which we cannot ansr wtout money from you

      All from yours   Henry Fogo   William Fogo"

Added " Mr Cowan here makes a heavie complaint you have not paid him ... am afraid youll find few fond of your Commissions tho I wish it were oyr ways".

Coline Campbell detailed his 1736 expenses including those concerning the *Black Bitch*:

    "April discussions about how to handle Hodge affair

    1st May Waiting on Capt Campbell (an advocate in Inveraray)

    Procuring his interest about ye *Black Bitch*   £1 - 15s

    14th June Shoaring Mr Cowans 6 hhds at Inver £2 - 0s

    8th July Incidents at meeting wt Archd Campbell

    at Connell   8d

    2nd August going to oban & staying a night

    wt A C re concerns of B B   4s - 6d

    16th August Express to oban wt ye letters brought

    by Geo: Stevenson   1s - 2d

16th August going & staying a night at oban
re ye Compy business wt AC   4s - 6d
30th August to ane express sent by Hodge from
Toppermorrie giving notice that he went to Noroway   6s - 0d
30th August to going to oban to consult AC what
was to be done   4s - 6d"

Captain Hodge had caused consternation when he returned to Oban in August 1736, presumably in another ship.   On 15th August Archibald Campbell, the Oban company manager, wrote from Oban to Coline Campbell "Ordered Hodge away before yours came and sent him to the horse shoe.   She was riding here when I came home. Collonsay is here and he wants much to see you. Hodge cannot with this wind go to the Sound of Mull but he should be ordered to some private place in the inner Sound. For gods sake come that we may concert what to do with her. I am afraid we will have a searcher here very soon and if she be lying in the way she may be searched".

                                                  (GD 1 / 2 9/10).

Before the end of August, Mr Hodge reached Tobermory from where he made a hurried departure for Norway.   He subsequently posed a threat to the partners of the Oban Company. The seizure at Airth on 29th February 1736, and a possible trial by the Commissioners, were frequently referred to as "the cursed bitch affair".

A year later, on 22nd June 1737. William Fogo was worried that Mr Hodge might soon be home from Norway.

Coline Campbell was absent from Inveresragan seeking a favourable outcome to the affair from 6th July to 17th August 1737 and claimed the following expenses

6th July 1737   Messrs Wm & Henry Fogo Drs to 2/3 of my personal
             charges ... Ednr Woodhall Gargunnock Alloa & Inveraray
             letters to solicite my friends to make interest at ye
             Commissioners of Customs to pass ye Debr due on ye Cargo
             of ye *Black Bitch* of Elphingstown. I was abroad from this
             date till ye 17th August including sundry drink money at same
             the whole expense   £22- 8s- 9d
             of this they pay 2/3rds as above
             to my extraordinary charges in buying cloaks wtout which
             I coud not appear at Ednr places and forgot. I had no
             occasion if not gone about ye affair & besides loss of time of
             Season   £13-14s- 7d

This was the second time Coline Campbell had renewed his wardrobe while engaged in company business, this time for the Oban company.

William Fogo also sought to avoid prosecution over the tobacco seized at Airth and he dealt with the legal side. On 5th August 1737 he wrote three long letters to Coline Campbell, who may have been in Falkirk on that day.

August 5th from Kilhorn:
" In answer to yours I go this day to Alloa and shall do all I can with that Collr tho am afraid to litle purpose for you know what a fickle gentleman he is tho perhaps Mrs Campbell may have some Influence with him ... cannot understand what Mr Ogilvie means by writing so, if it be not to gett himself clear of that bargain and force you and us all to relieve him ... after one hardship another tho wish it were ended that we might be more independant of him & join others".

August 5th from Alloa:
"Sir, I was with mr Campbell when yours came to him and one from Mrs Campbell to Mr Grossat which he is to deliver and think he will be prevailed with to make a favourable report ... tho he is so fickle I shall have my own fears ... make all dispatch to gett it ended ... the sooner the better for many reasons ... pray be as sparing of charges as possible (or) the remedy will be as ill as the disease. Jo: Campbell will write you ... take advice and do accordingly ... gett by all means a letter from Caldell and one from my Lord Cathcart to Grossat and some of ye Commrs and from Brigadier Jack Campbell ".

August 5th from Stirling (very emphatic writing!):
"Sir, Since writing my former and after taking a botle with Grossat and Campbell find him most precarious ... when he came to talk of the story ... he behoved to be paid for a report ... I find he aims att Great things £200 or 300 ... Jo: Campbell seems to mitigate him before me but he also is vastly greedie I told you if you took my advise before you gave Jon £50 you shoud stand by it so woud have you very cautious in treating with them particularly grossett he insists for it in hand tho I think ye client shoud determine and in that case only security shoud be granted and lodged with Jo: Campbell till the event and I will not coupt it above £40 att most tho I think £20 is a great deal.
referr it to K & K if he will take it on so converse him and be cautious at Alloa which way woud have you come home and call first for Jo: Campbell but confess nothing only to prevent charges he has promised not to report soon hoping you will make all dispatch, this sent by express to Falkirk".

Mr Fogo continued to write to Coline Campbell about the unresolved *Black Bitch* affair
On 18th January 1740:
"Your friends Sir Duncan and Mr Mcmillan are so obstinate that they woud do nothing in a friendly way ... am advised the bitch tryall will not come on this term ... hodge is at home his ship being frozen in tho

concerted with mr ogilvie ... nothing shoud be neglected to defeat their design
We have such froast here the lyke never knowen".
And on 6th February 1740:
"As for the *bitch* Mr Campbell who is with me tells there is to be no tryall this term ... shall do the best with hodge I can by another hand". The matter was still unresolved on 24th January 1743 when Mr Fogo wrote to Coline: "nothing yet got done with *bitch* debts: our old affairs must be put in some order. You know they lie in confusion". William Fogo was much concerned about the damage the evidence of Mr Hodge and his crew might do, should the matter come to Trial. It seems that the three partners lost £494-2s or £164-14s each. The seized tobacco, still unclaimed, was later ceremonially burned in public at Leith and there is no record of any trial having taken place.

The Oban Company

The Lochetty Company, which is well documented at Ardchattan, was dissolved on 26th April 1733 and apparently replaced on 20th July 1733 by a loose partnership of individuals who traded in their own names.   (appendix A)
Records in the Ardchattan Archives are mainly of incoming correspondence to Coline Campbell so that Oban affairs are seen only as far as they impinge on Inveresragan. There are, for example, no records of local trade from Oban, except for occasional purchases by Patrick McGrigor, the Oban merchant of long standing and by John McDougall of Dunollie, the Jacobite Chief who had been pardoned in 1727. John Campbell was Oban's boatman. He and "McAndra" at Bonawe carried most of the tobacco and wines to and from Loch Etive. There are many letters from Archibald Campbell, Manager at Oban, to Coline Campbell. These and other Oban documents are written on inferior paper and are difficult to read.

The Oban Company was formed at a meeting in Glasgow on 30th December 1734. The Minutes of partners' meetings are summarised at appendix A.   (GD 1/2/17 7/1-7/5)
The first partners were William and Henry Fogo and Archibald Gray, merchants in Glasgow. David Young was to be cashier at Glasgow and Archibald Campbell was to be manager or factor at Oban. He had arrived as "shopkeeper to Inveresragan & Co" in 1732 and may have been related to Coline Campbell because he sometimes signed his letters "yours affectionatlie" and made very occasional obscure family references – which may have been coded messages.
Archibald Gray was replaced almost immediately by Coline Campbell of Inveresragan, and these three initially each put in £100 sterling.
                                                        (appendix A)

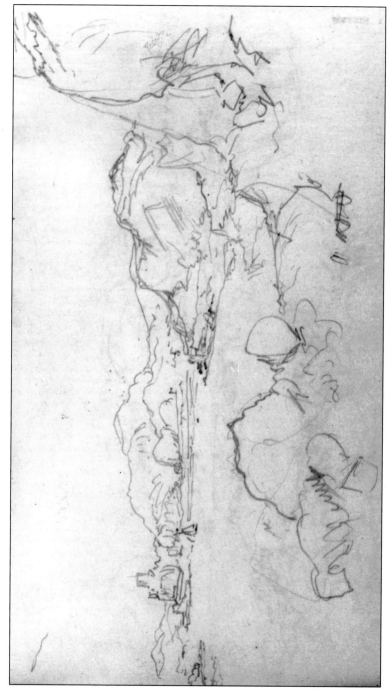

Oban Bay and Dunollie Castle. A sketch by J L W Turner, around 1818. © Tate, London 2004.

Some Oban people sketched by J L W Turner. © *Tate. London 2004*

More Oban people sketched by J L W Turner.   © Tate, London 2004

All the correspondence between the Fogo brothers and Coline Campbell in the archives at Ardchattan Priory indicate that these three men were equal and active partners in the first Oban company. William Fogo and Coline Campbell had had quarter shares in the earlier Lochetty company (along with Duncan Campbell of Inverawe and John Campbell of Lossit). Each Oban partner stood to gain one-third of profits earned by the Oban company and each was liable for one-third of subsequent losses. They also each bought one-quarter of the good ship *Diamond*, the other quarter being owned by the Master, Captain Robert Arthur. The one active sleeping partner was "Collonsa" (McNeill of Colonsay).

Neill Campbell of Achinard, mentioned in the first Oban contract, was involved in 1733 in the import of 753 bolls of meal mentioned in the draft contract. There was no record of the disposal of this purchase, which was to pose financial problems later. It is just possible that this meal had been imported in the *Nathaniel & John*, which was seized at Dunstaffnage in July 1732.

Cellars and a tobacco mill were built at Oban during 1735 and brought into use in conjunction with the facilities at Inveresragan. It appears that up to "four spinners and their servants" were employed at Oban, but half of them were laid off at one time.

The Oban merchant Patrick McGrigor ("his mark PMG") sent an account to Coline Campbell in 1735 for supplying "butter, 5 barrels herring at 14s each and 1 stone cheese for Alexr Clemie, Spinner". Mr Clemie, a spinner at Inveresragan, may have been in Oban then to set up the mill. (1 / 2 17 1/2/1)

On 19th February 1736 at a meeting at Lochgoilhead it was agreed to enlarge the Oban Company. It appears that six partners put £300 sterling into the New Oban Company They were

> Wm Fogo and Henry Fogo who each put in £300
> David Young who bought William Somervell's share but couldn't be assessed because he had supplied £158 of shop goods to Oban.
> Daniell McNeill of Colonsay who put in £300 less £198-2-1
> John MacLachlan, merchant in Fort William, who joined with £300
> Coline Campbell of Inveresragan who joined with £300
> Archibald Campbell, the Manager at Oban, may have contributed £150 of Coline's share.
> Archibald Gray was to be out when creditors for £100 had been repaid and Robert Arthur seems to have joined after he bought the *Diamond* in 1738.

The Oban partners decided to end the company at a partners' meeting in Oban on 2nd November1737, but it was then decided "to continue trading for a twelvemonth". Trading actually continued for a number of years at Oban, mostly under the names of the individual partners, and increasingly by employees Archibald Buchanan, John Nicolson and Matthew Simson acting in their own names as "merchants in oban". The tenuous trading link with Inveresragan was maintained and the tobacco mill there often rolled Oban tobacco until Coline Campbell of Inveresragan died in 1745. He had left the Oban Company some years before that date, but still owed money to the new Oban Company partners.

Coline Campbell appears to have paid his capital in the first Oban Company as follows. According to a memo dated 20th February 1736, he paid £51- 17- 11 to David Young presumably for shop goods, thereby reducing his capital by that amount. However it is noted that he paid the partnership a total of £319- 10- 4 in May and July 1736 and on 8th January 1737. Some time later he withdrew from Oban while continuing to trade on his own account at Inveresragan and to spin tobacco there for the Oban Company.

It is recorded that William Fogo had a share in shop goods sold at Oban from 19th April to 26th October 1736, but there are few details of local trade from Oban. (GD 1 / 2 1/ 4)

The Oban partners bonded all the cargoes of tobacco imported into Fort William Customs area from January 1736, sometimes as individuals and sometimes signing "for the old company".

It is not clear how much of the *Diamond*'s first cargo of January 1735, which was bonded at Alloa, reached Oban. William Fogo wrote to Coline Campbell on 5th May:

"lose no time till you go to fortwilliam and mind not to be extravagant in charges for that makes folk think you are getting favours".

William Fogo's letter of 5th May 1735 reads as follows:

"The gabert that is designed for oban goes wt coal to Ireland and if agreed to take in pilote att oban you could not afford to pay him ten or twelve pounds for your rungs tho I could sell you eight in all, yet do not see how you'll get him here".

This reference to rungs may be significant in locating the site of the Oban tobacco mill.

Within the Distillery, which was built much later, there is a landing stage with iron rungs for tying up vessels. This is today hidden behind a brick wall. According to the Minutes of the Oban Company the Oban mill was to be supplied from Fort William by a flat- bottomed craft capable of carrying 20 hogsheads. The Distillery site was part of Glencruittenmore, which the Oban Company leased for the tobacco mill and stores. There was also a water supply, which was later used by the distillery. All we can say for certain is that the Oban tobacco mill was north of the stream, now called the Black Lynn, which marked the southern boundary of the Glencruitten lands of Campbell of Dunstaffnage. It was not at the "ob" on the Duke of Argyll's Glenshellach estate, where the Customs House was built when it was moved from Fort William in 1760. The "ob" between the Railway and the South Piers, which gave Oban its name, is now infilled.

Mr Fogo intended to send 100 hogsheads of the second ¬January 1736- cargo to Oban from the Customs House at Fort William. The duty on the 300 hogsheads bonded there on this second voyage was £2,666 Sterling, half of which was payable on 8th July 1736. We hear no more of 30 hogsheads which were unloaded at Horseshoe Bay, Kerrera by pre-planned subterfuge, before the Diamond reached Fort William. This was earmarked for "Collonsa". The circumstances are detailed under "Captain Arthur and the *Diamond*".

Inter-company transactions are difficult to unravel, and some bills remained unpaid.
On 27th October 1736, Coline Campbell claimed expenses from the Oban Company due to the *Diamond's* January 1736 arrival at Fort William.
His waste book entries during 1737 read retrospectively:
"Donald MacAndrew & Crew brought tobacco from *Diamond*, January 1736" (to Oban)
"Drink money to Peter Cook my spinner"
"Incidents to freight Patersons Brig at oban"
Archibald Campbell at Oban wrote to Coline Campbell on 25th July 1736 "ordered the boat up to you with a good hhd and six mean".

There is a separate account dated 27th October 1736 detailing various amounts of leaf tobacco supplied during the year by Oban to Inveresragan at 2½d -3d per pound export prices. The details are:

June 1736 1 hhd	10th Aug 1 hhd	1623 lbs at 3d	£20- 5- 9
August 36 1 hhd	Nov 1 hhd	1494 lbs at 2 ¼ & 3d	£17- 2- 9
October36 2 hhds			£13-13- 5

The account reads:
"by *Diamonds* discharge 1735. Total, (as above) £51- 1- 11½
by Ship *Diamond* 1735 charges 21st May 1736 £ 1-16 - 0
by Archd Campbell, paid him 3rd May 1736 £18- 2- 1
3 snuff rolls, 109 lbs at 7d £ 3- 3- 7
and small amounts for madder, linnen, loaf sugar etc
The Oban Company was a debtor to
Inveresragan for 1/3rd of £131- 5- 2 £43-15 – 0¾

A considerable quantity of leaf tobacco was being "bought of the oban compy for Inveresragan for spinning" notably a list of numbered hogsheads totalling 60 hundredweights 2 quarters 25 pounds between 20th June 1736 and September 1737.

The corresponding amount of leaf tobacco rolled at Inveresragan from 5th June 1736 to 10th August 1737 was 80 cwts 1 qtr 7 ¼ lbs made up as follows:

5th June 36 to 28 July 36	17 cwts	2 qtrs	21 lbs
28th July 36 to 12th November 36	11 cwts	2 qtrs	9¾ lbs
12th November 36 to 21st January 37	9	0	7
21st January 37 to 21st February 37	5	3	13
21st February 37 to 15th March 37	1	2	0
15th March 37 to 25th March 37	1	3	27
25th March 37 ti 23rd May 37	13	0	10½
23rd May 37 to 10th August 37	19	2	13
total	80 cwts	1 qtr	7¼ lbs

In an account dated October 1737, the leaf tobacco sent from Oban for spinning in June, August, October, November 1736, and up to 15th August 1737, was charged at a total of £75-16s made up as follows: "by 4 lb allowed on the hhds   £ - 7s

by balance of capital	£17-17
by balance due by 2 bills	£57-12 total £75-16"

This account was updated in 1743 with the two bills totalling £57-12s, still unpaid as:

"Coline Campbell esq, Debtor
    To balance of above, viz:

11th Nov 1736 one bill payable 11/6/37	£ 19- 8 - 8
15th Aug 1737 2nd bill payable 15/3/38	£ 38- 3 - 4
total	£ 57-12
interest on first bill (above) to Feb 1743	£ 5- 8 - 6
interest on 2nd billdo	£ 9- 9 - 3
26th Jan 1739 to 3103 lbs tob: as per acct	£ 38-15 - 9
9th July 1740 to 4675 lbs tob:do	£ 60-17 - 5
to 14,591 lbs tob which is to be exported at 4d/lb	£243- 3 - 8
total	£415- 6 - 7
Creditor	
By leaf exported at 4d.	£231-17
By balance due to Company	£183- 9 - 7
total	£415- 6 - 7"

On 18th March 1738, Archibald Campbell wrote from Oban to Coline "receive two hhds tobacco for spinning and sending to the Low Country". He suggested a meeting at Bonawe "Be shure to be there very earlie and bring ane accot o the tobacco you got since the 1st October last". Coline's reply (undated) was:
    "tobacco sent from Oban to Inveresragan (GD 1 / 2 2/4)

16th November 1737	3 cwts	0 qtrs	0 lbs	by Mcandras boat
10th December 1737	12	0	11	gott at Dunstaffnage
30th January 1738	16	2	3	
18th March 1738				
1 hogshead	5	1	15	
1 hogshead	8	2	14"	

On 29th April 1738 Coline Campbell was with the partners in Glasgow, including Colonsay, and he was seeking tobacco to spin. He may have left the Oban company by that date. The following note was written in Coline's own hand:

"Its resolved by the oban Compy that 5 hhds sufficient leaf tob for spinning be delivered to Coline Campbell of Inveresragan at oban without delay by Archd Campbell the manager as he shall give most advisable for the company and the said Colines Interests one at Inland sale price and four for Export because the sd Colines last parcell bought of Sd company was very mean. (Signed by) The Subscribers Coline Campbell   Donald McNeill (Colonsay)   David Young   Henry Fogo".

This delivery did not take place and when he returned to Inveresragan Coline wrote to the Oban Company to complain. The undated copy letter, in Coline's own hand, reads:
"Gentlemen   (GD 1 / 2 9/12)
You may all remember that on the 29th april last, the whole Company ... appointed Archd Campbell to deliver me forth with 5 hhds leaf tobacco one at inland rates and four Exports ... but Mr Campbell was Countermanded by you at Glasgow therby my work was stopt my Customers Disapointed, Spinners and Strappers Idle and wages to pay. If this be fair Dealling I Leave the world to Judge.
Pray order Mr Campbell to furnish me leaf to keep my work going".

On 20th May 1738 Archibald Campbell in Oban wrote apologetically to Coline:
"About your tobacco they cut me of from giving you any for there is very little good to spin". In the same letter Archibald goes on: "Archd Campbell att Crinan means to buy some tobacco of me. I hear he is not safe to be trusted so advise me whether you know any thing about him and if I can trust him. The tobacco is my own as you know I can sell him none of the company   Yours affectionatlie Archd Campbell".

The Oban store was used by William Fogo to hold or transfer much larger quantities of tobacco for sale in the Lowlands.
An account dated October 1738 of "tob: belonging to oban co and sent to be accompt for by Mr Fogo and Mr Young" lists the following:
"Tobacco at Down (Doune) & oyr places belonging to ye company unexported in Oct. 1738 to be Exported towards clearing & sent coast wise to Glasgow   36,275 libs

Computed at oban, Fort wm   40,000 libs
                     total   76,278 libs
Credit at Glasgow or Barrastowness (Bo'ness)   57,061 libs
Balance to Ship on ye Credit at Ft wm
                  net total   19,217 libs
Stock in ye oban Company after paying all debts except ye Contrlls
£3,297- 4- 1"
Much of this tobacco was carried overland from Oban by pack-horse
(see below).

An account of February 1743 gives in 1739, 3482 lbs
sold at 3 1/8ᵗʰd for   £45- 6- 9
And in July 1740 of 2 hhds –some replaced- of 1193 lbs
sold at 3 1/8ᵗʰd at   £15-10-8
            Total   £60-17-5
This whole account is titled "Tob trade Coline Campbell of
Inveresragan to Oban Compy". Relating to this account there was a
"Scheme of the Exchange to be charged the new oban compy between
1738 and 1740". This four- page document is hard to read.

Coline Campbell's expenses claims from May 1739 to February 1741
were small and were mostly incurred in the shop and local trading.
One interesting entry of 15ᵗʰ May 1739 shows that the spinners at
Inveresragan did sometimes work under pressure. It reads: "A bottle
whisky to the lads rolling out 6 hhds under night at Inver".

Archibald Campbell wrote to Coline Campbell from "oban october ye
13ᵗʰ 1739:
I have sent you by the bearer a hhd of the best tobacco I had and as
many bottels as I can spare. Customs paper is not come here as yet
soe shoon as it does shall send it to you. John McLachlane writes me
that some day shoon Collector McNeill is to be att your house and
heare. I doe not believe that he will meddle but open noe doors to
him".
Added:
"send me the accot settled with McAndrew (the boatman at Bonawe).
I shall be readie shoon to go to the Low Country … I am now going
throw all the books … wish you would come here on Friday next and
you would get a double of your accots from the beginning to this day".

And from "oban october ye 21ˢᵗ 1739
I have given Mr Mcfarlane a double of all your tobacco accots which
compare with Mr Peter (Cook, a spinner) and youll see its right youll
likewise see by accot what leaf is in my hand   all the roall you sent
down are sold to the Strontian people but that from Isla is upon hand
and I cannot tell what to doe with it   you may have candles and Stems

I cannot now send you the accot of the wine and shugar but shall bring it up with me ... I shall be att your house when I will goe to the Low Country ... there is a veshell to be round this week and to morrow morning I send ane express to Clyde to order some things round in her for myself.

You shall have Credit with the Oban Company for your accot of wine and shugar. I will take none of it in my accot as it was layed out on there accot its as proper they pay it as I doe".

Duncan McVicar, Merchant in Maryburgh

Archibald Campbell, Manager of the Oban company, wrote to Coline Campbell from Connel, on 24th April 1737:

"Dear sir

I forgot when I seed you last to speak to you about ane affair that I am to be concerned in at Fort william

The affair is this. Duncan McViccar is goeing to drop the Excise and to set up shoap keeping ... he made ane offer to me of a share which I have promised to be concerned   I mean to put in ane hundred pounds with him ... John McLachlane is to drop his shoap and is to joyn: the Governour putts in for him if he does not and McLachlane is not in the list to be concerned in receiving the Cash or making any bargains ... Duncan Mcviccar is to have the whole management ... I think realie it most unsure – I promised to speak to you they want you concerned let me know your opinion of it by the first oportunity ... I am to put in one sixth sterling and they are to buy there tobacco of me ... I have joyned Robine Arthur in his tobacco and can make something by providing them with tobacco ... if you incline to be concerned you may goe hands with me in what tobacco I provide them with.

Duncan McViccar will be down shoon and will speak to you about it and will tell you the whole affair as I am in heast have no more but that I am

          yours affectionatlie arch"

added

"Doe not show this to Duncan McVicar for he may then think I have ane design that I am to trick him with the tobacco".

Duncan McVicar became an important merchant in Fort William and he may have been involved in the very large cargo of tobacco and iron, which was shipwrecked off Lismore in 1742. There was also an Oban connection in that affair (see below).

Captain Robert Arthur and the *Diamond*

By 1734, Robert Arthur was Master of the *Diamond* and owned a quarter share. He may then have been aged about thirty. The other quarters were bought in 1734 by William & Henry Fogo and by Coline Campbell of Inveresragan. In that year Captain Arthur left from Berwick with 'a sorted cargo' for Cadiz. There he loaded salt for Virginia and brought back 297 hogsheads of leaf tobacco to Airth on the Forth early in January 1735. This was bonded at Alloa Custom house by William Fogo and others in the newly-formed Oban Company.

William Fogo wrote from Alloa on 21 January 1735 to Coline Campbell:

"We are now going on but sadly plagued by that Scoundrell from Greenock oyrwise all woud a been very discreet: but there's noe helping of that oppression.

The new (Oban) Compy will not want a brigg for six months, then we may buy her. Gett Achinard to Join you for £300 and I will gett you in, that is £150 each, you both standing one share. The Certificate for the 20 thousand ex-*Diamond* ... I know you want tobacco to spin: pray remitt any money if you have or can gett it soe to pay the last freight ... take care the Debentur be right done".

Mr Fogo had warned Coline Campbell that the *Diamond* might touch at Dunstaffnage or Horseshoe Bay on its way to Airth, though not insured for the West coast. If it did, the tobacco spinner Clemie and another man may have laid information against the partners. In a letter dated 5th March 1735 William Fogo writes: "As for Clymie I cannot find him out ... my broyr goes this week and will enquire about him further". And on 31st March "As for Clymy am told he was att Glasgow lately and keept himself private: but now is gone to Whitehaven or Liverpool ... if soo may be found out but he is a sad villain. There is a caption against Hugh the oyr villain and he absconds but cannot live here. He is now a bellman".

The second voyage of the *Diamond* returned in January 1736 for the first time direct to Fort William Customs House. Archibald Campbell, Manager of the Oban company, was on the ship. There was a prearranged plan to offload 30 hogsheads of leaf tobacco at Horseshoe Bay before the ship reached the Customs House.

In preparation, William Fogo wrote from Glasgow to Coline Campbell on 15th November 1735: "We desire you'll be so kind as to go to Fort William and procure houses or cellars for the *Diamond*'s cargo when she arrives. Think it may be towards the end of December before she comes in and no doubt must lay until the Commissioners are advised. Her loading will be 330 hogsheads but you are to reckon on 300 and call her burden no more: for its designed that 30 hhds be put out before the entry and the report to be that short. Must depend on Collonsa and you to manage at the Custom House".

(signed)   William Fogo   David Young
Added: "take care this comes into no other hand than your own – you may show it (only) to Collonsa".

On the same day, 15th November 1735, William Fogo and David Young – not for the first time - invited Coline Campbell to invest in the new Oban Company by paying £300 sterling, or securing credit for the same sum towards the Customs Duties when the Diamond returned. They wrote: "signify your Complyance by a missive and you shall be adjoined and the copartnery sent up for you to sign ... we after knowing your mind shall write you of amount of the whole cargo and whats intended Collonsa has one Double".
At this time Coline Campbell joined the Oban company in place of Archibald Gray, who may have become bankrupt.

On his return from Virginia, Archibald Campbell wrote to Coline Campbell from "the horseshoe" on 31st December 1735.
"By this know of our safe arrival here on (Sunday) 28th instant. Next morning I went ashore to Mr Nicolson" (Clerk at Oban) "where I received a letter from the oban company att Glasgow advising me to call for you and carrie you to Fort william and as we are here now and have severall things on board that will not stand the test, wish that att the receipt of this you would come here or meet me at oban that you may advise whether it be proper to land them here or there. I design in the morning to send a Boat for Collonsa finding by theres that the entrey cannot be made without him ... wishing you a good new year from your most humble Servt   Archibald Campbell"
Added below:
"Thursday morning being disappointed of the express last night thought fit to add that parting our Cable when we came to ane anchor we drove ashore but are gotten off then we took out a boats load to lighten her it is now in the boat soe I wish you would make all heast that I might know whether to take it on board again or not. I shall not send to Collonsa till I heare from you".

The ship was certainly partly unloaded at Horseshoe Bay on Kerrera. The driving ashore incident resulted in legal proceedings at the Admiralty Court at Inveraray against another ship as early as 2nd January 1736. A petition in the name of Robert Arthur "for himself & in the name of Neill Campbell of Achinard, John Nicolson merchant in Oban and partners of the Oban Company" sued that Robert Paterson & James Kirkwood, master of the other ship be summoned.   It was claimed that these men ordered the Diamond's cable to be cut when it was taut against the side of their ship and placing it in danger. As a result "the Diamond was driven forcibly on shore and could not be got off for several days".   (Bigwood - AC 20/2/6 of 1736)

On January 5th 1736 a letter in William Fogo's hand was also signed by David Young and Henry Fogo, and it was addressed to Messrs Coline Campbell of Inveresragan, Donald Mcneil of Colonsa and Jo: Mclachlan, merchant in fort william. It reads:

"Gentlemen   (GD 1/2/17)

Being advised by the master that the shipe *Diamond* is now arrived at horseshoe and is ordered for fort william we must depend on you to manadge the whole affair there and offer herein our best advice viz that you go to fort william with the master or before him and concert his repport as he will give you acct which is necessary to be done: and after that is done offer to make an entry of 300 hhds att 600 (lbs) and by that you'll know how they use you, if the Collr refuses ane entry you are to protest and he is to send ane express to the Commrs advising you have done so and to send a copy of the protest concluding with damnages in case the shipe and cargo shall be damnified ... Angus Mcneil who is here has written them advising her arrival and design: but by no means is the Collr to discharge without advising them ... tho he might and we coud force that

out of regard to him do not think it expedient   I am credibly informed from Edn that one or two will be sent up and Jo: Campbell from Alloa probably one, so its proper to have the report and entry made before that ... that there be no delay for you can expect no favours so do your best: so at least the report might be made you are to bond this cargo and satisfie the Collr as to the security of what you enter and as it is discharged it is to be qualified and 60 hhds of the best quality sent by the shipe *diamond* to this store which you shall have our conjunct obligation to be accountable if sold for export or inland consumpt for the whole nate proceeds ... you need not scrouple your bonding for you may be satisfied we intend nothing but fare dealing all the tob: must be weyed att fortwilliam and cellared and then incline 100 hhds be sent to oban and sixty to this and the rest keept att fortwilliam ... we design to order up a lighter with all necessary ... in regard several other things may be needfull we leave it intirely to your prudent management and pray dispatch

we are your humble servts William Fogo David Young Henry Fogo" added:

"The tob: must be entered and the shipe dispatched for another voyage to sail sometime in march".

The amount of leaf tobacco entered at Fort William in January 1736 was 297 hogsheads weighing 217,076 lbs, which indicates that about 30 hogsheads were unloaded at Horseshoe Bay in Kerrera "for Collonsa" before the *Diamond* reached Fort William.

The disposal of the cargo during 1736 is listed in a subsequent account as follows:

"Feb:	shipped coastwise to Clyde	49,784 lbs
	exported in the *Diligence* (19th March)	88,500 lbs
July:	exported in the *Robert & Ralph* of Newcastle	42,820 lbs
	(cleared for Campvire on 14th July 1736)	
	sent coastwise to Liverpool	4,409 lbs
	exported to Ireland in the *Agnes*	3,238 lbs
	exported in the *Sally*	1,701 lbs
	exported in the *Lyon of Irvine*	6,225 lbs
	ditto	9,237 lbs
	exported in the *Providence*	2,114 lbs
	by the *Recovery* of Fort William	2,140 lbs
	total	210,168 lbs"

It appears that there was a ready market for the cargo, but some of the "exports" may have been relanded at Oban, Inveresragan, Colonsay or other places.

The New Oban Company was already in financial difficulties in 1737. The partners decided to end the company but to continue manufacture and disposal "for a twelvemonth". This was to deal with the leaf tobacco already landed from the *William & John* and with the cargo of the *Diamond*, when it would arrive.at the end of the year. Meanwhile two of the four tobacco spinners at Oban were to be dismissed and there was to be no voyage of the *Diamond* in 1738. The Glasgow partners were authorised to decide whether or not to sell the *Diamond*.

The Glasgow partners decided to sell the *Diamond* when Captain Arthur was on his third voyage to Virginia but he was back in time to attend the auction at Glasgow.
William Fogo and David Young wrote to Coline Campbell on 10th March 1738.
"This day we rouped the shipe *Diamond* when there were several bidders and particularly Mr Dreg(h)orn and some adhering to him did bid £345 and Mr Arthur at the run of the glass gott her for £353 Dreg(h)orn declaring he had no orders to go further than £350: so now she is Mr Arthurs and to prevent any grumbling or reflections doubt not but we can prevail with him to let you or any or all of the former partners and owners having a share if you think her too low or Incline to be concerned as we propose to take a share with him but we have stipulate that any concerned shall stand in shipe and cargo and have a man here of character and probite to Join in buying and paying the cargo & outrigg with the partners here".
Captain Arthur, who was now the dominant figure in the partnership, set sail again for Virginia on 18th April 1738 with a new crew and a supercargo named John Muschet.
Not long after he returned, the Oban company minutes record on 10th

May 1739 that Robert Arthur and company was re-engaging the two spinners and their servants who had been laid off at Oban "because two spinners were too few for such a large house and utensils". On his part, Captain Arthur agreed not to sell tobacco to the Oban Company's customers.

From 1734 to 1743 Robert Arthur completed at least eight round voyages in the *Diamond* carrying goods across the Atlantic for sale in Virginia and Maryland and bringing back cargoes of up to 100 tons of leaf tobacco to Scottish ports. At least six return voyages were made direct to Fort William Customs House between January 1736 and 1743.

The voyages of January 1735 to Airth and of January 1736 to Fort William have been detailed above. The next recorded dates of bulk imports of leaf tobacco are:

January 1737: 215,677 lbs in 287 hogsheads taken to Fort William in the *Diamond*

October 1737: 94,160 lbs landed at Fort William from the *William & John* of Irvine.

The 1737 total of 309,837 lbs was bonded by Donald McNeill of Colonsay, John MacLachlan of Fort William, Archibald Campbell, Coline Campbell, David Young (also for William Somervell) and William Fogo (also for Henry Fogo).   (GD 1 / 2 17 9/18)

In January 1738, 173,050 lbs were landed at Fort William from the *Diamond* and bonded at £3,267-18-10 by Coline Campbell, Archibald Campbell, John MacLachlan and Robert Arthur.

An undated copy of a 1738 letter from Coline Campbell is in the files addressed to "Fogo & oban company". It reads:

"Gentlemen, I received yours advising of your being undetermined where to Discharge the *Diamond*. I wish in the first place she was safely arrived for the place of entry is no great matter to me tho certainly fort william is most convenient. The colleague at oban might be kept on ye old footing till may or june for spinning ye 50 hhds or as much of them as can be done. I can see no difficulty in sending down by land the 50 hhds".

In the event the Diamond did sail to Fort William Custom House.

On 1st January 1739, 57 hogsheads of leaf tobacco – 44,688 lbs - were bonded by four partners. They were David Young, William and Henry Fogo and Robert Arthur. This total was later reduced to 52 hogsheads of 39,607 lbs on which the Customs Duty was £748-2-5.

On 8th January a further bond for 176 hogsheads of leaf tobacco weighing 137,984 pounds was entered into at the Custom House by all six (or seven) partners in the Oban company. According to a later legal document they were Donald McNeill, John MacLachlan, Archibald Campbell and Coline Campbell, David Young (and for

William Somervell) & William Fogo. They paid £431 and bonded for £2,606 Sterling apparently "for the old company". This total was later reduced to 133,252 lbs on which the Duty was £2,573-2-4.

An independent document gives the Oban partners as: William Fogo, Henry Fogo, David Young, Donald McNeil of Colonsay, John MacLachlan of Greenhall, Archibald Campbell and Coline Campbell.

(Dell, SRO B10/15/6021)

A reproachful letter from Archibald to Coline in 1740, seems to show that Archibald and Coline shared a sixth share, the whole of which fell to Archibald when Coline withdrew from the New Oban company.

Coline Campbell invoiced the New Oban Company for the following expenses:

"Jany 1739: to my charges going to and at Fort Wm attending the Discharge of the *Diamonds* cargo & Bonding the same £5- 5- 7 to cash pd Donald McAndrew Boatman, for freight on accot of sd compy £3-17- 6".

Coline Campbell played a major part in bonding this cargo, but there is no subsequent record of major transactions at Inveresragan, so it is likely that the Fogo brothers, David Young and Captain Arthur dealt with Coline Campbell only when they needed him.

In 1740 another cargo of tobacco was brought to Fort William in the *Diamond*. The only reference to this at Inveresragan is an Oban Company letter to Coline of 27th October 1740. "Captain Arthur has not passed this place yet".

From an unverified reference, Captain Arthur made another voyage to Virginia in 1741, but as there is no record of this in the Inveresragan papers, it is not known where the tobacco was landed.

(SRO SC51.48.14)

The last cargo known to be delivered direct to Fort William from the *Diamond* was in 1743. On 18th October, 123 hogsheads marked FY (Fogo-Young) were bonded in equal quarters by William & Henry Fogo, David Young and Robert Arthur, while 178 hogsheads were bonded "by the others" including John MacLachlan and Archibald Campbell. This cargo totalled 301 hogsheads. Coline Campbell did not attend that bonding but he was later involved when some of this cargo was to be secretly taken to Oban. In a letter to Coline dated 18th October 1743, Archibald Campbell, who was now in Glasgow, wrote:

"I am glad to know that you got safe home ... as to the manadgement of the ship with the tobacco Mr Arthur & I design to send her a Clearance to goe to the Garison with it and then shall bring it doun again to oban to you but if the Custom house people have seen her att all that will not answer soe in that event you are not to meddle with your tobacco till mr Mclachlane takes out his att the same time as he may be fessed if bulk broak.

I sent off your letter to Mr Gordon and I shall write you further by post.

If you want tobacco till yours returns you may apply to John Nicolson (at Oban)
send me by the bearer my black coat and pray get the Rum money in
Is all, sir   your most humble servt Archd Campbell".

Overland Deliveries of Tobacco to the Lowlands

Tobacco was delivered overland by pack-horse to merchants in the Lowlands, and especially during 1737 and 1738, from Oban. Some of these deliveries, usually of 1000 lbs at a time, are noted in the Inveresragan shop day-books, others by letter. Typically a pack horse was loaded with a balanced pack of two English hundredweights, each of 112 pounds. These were sometimes described as "hundred long weight" to distinguish them from packs of 200 lbs.

There were men around Loch Etive and Oban who had pack horses for hire including Dugald McColl, John McColl, John McNiven and Dugald McCallum at Kilmaronaig, Donald Gray at Connel, Duncan and Hugh McColl in Achavaich, near Oban and (in 1744) Duncan McKillop, carrier at Oban. These men would be very familiar with the trade by pack horse through Dalmally. This trade was purposeful and efficient, unlike the meanderings of the cattle drovers, who made their own way through the glens to the lowland markets.

The Pass of Brander must have been difficult to traverse. In January 1733 Coline Campbell "took Journey to Edinburgh and Glasgow with two horses and a brake". It is just possible that a track through the Pass could take a wheeled brake at this early date, but there are also references to boats on Loch Awe "from Brandre to Drissaig" while John McBain is recorded as "ferrier in Inistrynish" in 1740.

After Dalmally the tobacco was carried through Glen Lochy to Tyndrum or onward through Strathfillan to Killin. John Campbell had horses for hire at Tyndrum while Mungo Campbell was the contact at Killin. At these places the Highlanders sometimes handed over to various members of the Drummond family of Stirling who took the loads onward to Doune, Stirling, Perth, Falkirk or Bo'ness.

The following deliveries have been compiled from many documents.

1734	9,485lbs to Callander in total. In August it was intended to send 28 hogsheads of leaf and 51 rolls, calculated at 14 rolls per hogshead. Perhaps deliveries fell short of this, or the record is incomplete.
1735	17,901 lbs in total: details include:
7th April	3 hogsheads of leaf tobacco to John Cowan of Stirling
14th April	3 more hogsheads leaf to John Cowan
29th May	1200 lbs leaf to John Cowan by John Wright, carrier

n Stirling.

3rd July	900 lbs leaf to Robt Campbell of Torry by Duncan & Hugh McColl in Achaviach, by Oban
5th July	800 lbs leaf to John Cowan by Wm Drummond, carrier in Stirling
17th July	1200 lbs leaf to William Fogo by Wm Drummond, and 2400 lbs leaf to William Fogo by Duncan & Hugh McColl
5th August	1600 lbs leaf to John Cowan by Wm Drummond
15th August	12 hogsheads leaf to William Fogo at Killin - 48 horse loads
26th August	4 packs leaf to William Fogo "2 hundred long each pack".

A letter from Mr Fogo dated 15th August 1735 tells Coline how to deal with the major delivery that summer: "Think you should order this 10 to Killin so as to make 48 (packs) to auger the 12 hogsheads. Send 5 by Drummond and cause him to take the other 5 to Drysoch".

1736 7,952 lbs total   Overland deliveries in the summer of 1736 were as follows:

23rd June	1600 lbs leaf to William Fogo by Wm Drummond
1st July	12 packs leaf by William Fogo to be delivered 6 to Robert Campbell of Torry by Drummond 6 to Mckeanstons at Lochend and 1600 lbs to Torry by Duncan McColl in Achavaich.
29th July	10 packs leaf (2000 lbs) to Torry by Donald Gray at Connel
2nd August	20 cwts leaf in 10 packs to Torry by John McNiven, John McColl & Dugald McCallum in Kilmaronaig (Loch Etive).
1737	32,032 lbs to Doune per Oban Company 37,044 lbs per Oban giving an Oban Company total of 69,076 lbs, including 17 packs totalling 3,808 lbs which were owned by Robert Arthur.

The 1736 deliveries are more detailed than in other years. The total is itemised as:
11th June 7 cwts: 23rd June 16 cwts: 30th June 16 cwts: 1st July 24 cwts: 5th July 8 cwts. The total is 71 cwts x 112 lbs which is equal to 7,952 lbs

That this traffic was illegal and clandestine can be judged by the selling price to Lowland merchants of about 6d per pound and from the following detailed instructions from William Fogo to Coline Campbell of Inveresragan in a letter dated 26th June 1736:

"Send six (packs) by Drummond and your sixteen for the roll which will fill 6 hogsheads. Order all the rest to Torry where Robert Campbell has a barn provided and an honest fellow to Keep the Key. Put into each pack 2:0:0" (i e two hundredweights per horse) "Send down 20 at once or a dozen and give the charge to one you can trust." Mr Fogo's indirect route to Torry, near Doune,. is then detailed as follows:

"At tombae(?) through the water there to the south side and cross again at Bocastle and through the skirt of the moor to Torry. Would have you at Torry at 2 in the morning and by this youll miss Callander I mean Kilmahog. You and Archie must pay all the carriers from the highlands and I shall satisfy Drummond".

On July 4th 1736 Archibald Campbell wrote from Oban to Coline Campbell:

"I received yours by Dougall and have packed the twelve packs you sent me and design att twelve of the Clock this night to send off eight and the rest to morrow night.

I doe not see how I can send you the boat the *Diamond* being in the Country I am afraid it may be told him by some body or other that we are carrying tobo up and down the Country and provost Fishers meall Ship lyes at the door soe as we cannot get out without there knowledge but I take care they see nothing of the packs by packing them in the house. There is now gone and ready to goe near nineteen rolls which I think is enough att a time untill it be carried to Airth and then you may send the rest.

Send me by the bearer one of the bundles of the roap the four pack sheets that are already cutt and 29 yards of the harn to make Celtic Clouts for them and four packs from roall. I Design to send of eight packs of roall. Have noe more but that I shall see you of on Tuesday morning and that I am your most humble servant

Archd Campbell"

There was evidently a shortage of packing materials in 1736. On 19th July William Fogo wrote to Coline Campbell from Torry Ferry: "I came here this morning and there is 20 packs packed up but are hindered for want of packs. None can be gott att Glasgow I find we can have our own done with their cariage as cheap, so desire you send down four horse loads which will make 10 hhds (of packing) and cause them carry the sleaves in hochims or bundles with leathers and putt the heads and bottoms in a sack and lay them over betwixt on the horse back you'll gett them carried for 6s 8d or 7s at most I am sure you can load four horses and have written Archie to send other four horse loads and count 28 glabos to each hhd".

"Pray gett your accts soon ended and as much money as you can and remitt me less or more by Drummond I pay Drummond & partners to gett from oban 4 hhds soe that some may be sent from your place   If Archie be not returned think you shoud go to oban and see the tob: sent down" (a note on the sleeve) "go to oban and gett a good hhd and send down 4 packs of it to Drummond and mark it with a cross No 4 and order him to carry it to stirling".

The tobacco came from Oban to Inveresragan mostly in leaf form for spinning there or elsewhere, and Mr Fogos letters indicate that the trade was duty free. The main buyers were Robert Campbell of Torry, John Cowan of Stirling, John Ogilvy of Airth and Robert Christie of Stirling.

Trade between Oban and Inveresragan was a two-way flow.   In November 1738, Coline Campbell sold 63 export rolls from Oban inland at 7d per lb. The total was 1299 lbs and the rolls were sold for £37-13-9.

At some time during 1739, Coline Campbell bought 60 small rolls of tobacco from the Oban company – totalling 701 lbs 9 ozs, an average of only about 11 lbs per roll.

It was unusual for Coline to buy rolled tobacco from Oban. He mostly bought leaf to roll at Inveresragan. The amounts of leaf tobacco which were supplied by Oban to be rolled at Inveresragan between June 1739 and September 1740 are clearly laid out in the first seven pages of an account book.   (GD 1 / 2 7/6)

"20th June 1739 Received from oban by Invers boat, 2 hhds leaf
No 51 gross 7cwts 3qtrs 16lbs tare 2qtrs 27lbs neat 7cwts 0qtrs 17 lbs
No 27 " 8 " 0 " 6 " tare 3 " 3 " neat 7 " 1 " 3 "
One broken hhd leaf of a meaner quality of 5 cwts nearly
30 October 39 then received from oban
                    I broke hhd leaf 4 cwts 0 qtrs 9 lbs"
Elsewhere the total for 1739 is 3,482 lbs sold at 3d for £45- 6- 9.
"13th June 1740 received from oban 1 hhd leaf 7 cwts 2 qtrs 8 lbs
27th June 1740 received from oban 2 hhds leaf
                    No132 7 " 1 " 4 "
                    No124 6 " 2 " 19 "
25th Aug 1740 received from oban 1 hh No145 5 " 2 " 24 "
29th Sept 1740 received from oban
                    per parks Boat 1 hhd 7 " 3 " 14 "
        All except the last entry were sold in rolls from
                17th June up to 25th August 1740
Elsewhere the total for 1740 is 4,675 lbs sold at 3d for £60-17-5.
During this period 1739-40 leaf was exported from Oban at 4d per lb
                    for £231-odd
And on 23rd Dec 1740 it was planned to export on 1st Feb 1741, 2633 lbs at 3d or 3¼d

There is a version of the above which uses the nett totals (GD 1/2 2/4)

"20th June 1739   No 47 4 cwts 0 qtrs 0 lbs

" "   floor   1 cwt

18th July "	2 hhds	No 51	7 "		0 "		17 "	
		No 27	7 "		1 "		3 "	
3rd October 39		1 hhd	4 "		0 "		9 "	
total			23 "		2 "		1 "	

equals 2633 lbs

discount   12 lbs

total   2621 lbs

half at 3¼ per lb 1311 lbs	£17-15- 0¾
half at 3d per lb 1310 lbs	£16- 7 -6
old Subsidy of 2133 at ¾d	£ 8- 4- 6¾
interest to 1st January 1741	£ 6- 1
total	£42-13- 2½

23rd December 1740 "to grant obligation to export ye same 2633 agst 1st Febry and pay interest from 1st Janry next".

There are no later details of this overland supply of duty-free tobacco to the Lowlands.

A Customs Seizure near Mull

An incident which shows that other smugglers were active in the Firth of Lorn is described in a "Complaint and Petition" dated 29th March 1736. The complaint reads:

"That Robert Hunter, Shipmaster in Irvine (was) on Wednesday last 24th March 1736 under sail making for the sound of Mull on his voyage to Norway. James Savage officer of his majesties Excise in the Division of Lorn did with a party of armed men board the plaintiff, opened his hatches, Rummaged his hold and not only seized some brandy contained in a clearance for Norway, alleging that the petitioner had landed some part thereof in the said sound, saying the quantity Seized did not answer that in the Clearance. But brought his vessel to anchor in the Bay of Duart and time detained him and took away his cocket: to his great detrement and damage being under Charter party with merchants against which the said Robert Hunter protested at the Mast and required to be immediately Dismissed. Otherwise the said James Savage might not only be liable to him for the value of the brandy seized at 6 shillings and 8 pence per gallon but for all expences and damages he has or may sustain through the Illegal Seizure and Detaining of his vessel".

(He made oath) "that no part of brandy in the said cocket was relanded or put aboard any vessel ... he designs to proceed on his voyage and craves that the above protest may be marked. (signed) Robert Hunter"

"James Savage being present insisted that the Seizure was legal but he was willing to dismiss Mr Hunter upon his making an affidavit in terms of his written complaint."   (signed) Jas Savage

"Robert Hunter being solemly sworn ... depones that he has not by himself relanded any brandy in Scotland, England or the Isle of Man ... nor put it aboard any vessel in order to be relanded". (signed) Robert Hunter

There must have been an element of 'tongue in cheek' in these proceedings which were conducted at Inveresragan by Justices of the Peace – none other than - Duncan Campbell of Inverawe and Coline Campbell of Inveresragan.   Robert Hunter was not unknown to the two Justices, while Mr Savage, being based near Oban, was a frequent customer of the shop at Inveresragan.

Fictitious exports?
In 1737 the *Peggy* of Achindown sailed for Holland with 27,592 lbs of leaf tobacco.
There is an account dated October 1737 of the cost of this voyage, which may not have been to Holland.   (GD 1 / 2 2/3)

"to freight	£40	advanced by Wm Fogo	£20
to cash to sundries	£ 5	" by Archd Campbell	£30-15
to fees to Collector	£ 1- 5	" by company	£ 6-10
to fees to Surveyor	10		
Archd Campbells charge	£ 2- 10		
+ small items total	£57- 5	total	£57- 5
underneath this account			
Wm Fogo & Compy share	13,264 lbs		
		to C C share proportioned	£18- 6- 6
Robin Arthur	10,000 lbs		
		to Wm & Henry Fogo	£18- 6- 6
Coline Campbell	4,328 lbs		
		to Robin Arthur	£21- 2
Total	27,592 lbs	total	£57-15"

In May 1738, 2859 lbs were exported in the *Margaret* and 3 hogsheads of 2128 lbs in "the sloop". In July 1738 1200 lbs of roll were exported in the *Nancy* and in April 1739 one hogshead of 628 lbs was exported in the *Fortune* of Irvine.

John Paterson, Merchant in Renfrew
During 1736 and 1737 Coline Campbell had been legitimately selling

fir timber to John Paterson of Rathmellon, merchant in Renfrew, whose Skipper was named Smith.

One example is:

17 tons 10 cwts square timber at 22s per ton   £19- 5- 3

The total bill to Mr Paterson was £61- 0- 6.   This was met by Mr Paterson supplying Inveresragan with Linen, soap, 16 barrels of salt and other items from Ireland.

On 28th July 1738 Archibald Campbell of Oban wrote from Fort William to Coline.

"I was surprised to have the Inclosed from Mr Paterson. He is gone and am afraid that I have got a bite he certainly cannot be past Lochdon or esdale. I wish to ... stoop him I think you may detain him with ane admirall precept from Airds as I am engadged for severall times with him and I am afraid that I have meet with ... considering the letter he wrote me when att Airds".

Added:

"receive a paper with my name signed blank soe as you may send it to the admirall"

(There was a blank sheet enclosed, which was signed "Archd Campbell").

John Paterson's letter was addressed to "Mr Archd Campbell mercht att oban and dated

from "Dunstaffness 6 July 1738". It reads as follows:

"your very satirick letter I seed and thank you greatly; and shall endeavour to be greatful for such a singular instance of generosity. They told me I must await your return from Fort william but was obliged to take the fair wind soe you'll please to write to me what things I'll bring or send for your Herring fishing. My Bro: will require it of me he being Equailly Concerned in the vessell. You accuse me with what I never was accusd by any one else; its Certain a Continued Succession of misfortunes has followd me since I left home & I may also say since I had any dealings in the Highlands but cant accuse you of being cause of any had I taken your advice. Fisher served me as you told me he woud; very ungenerously ... youll please order down to oban what Casques are at Inveresragan of mine . Mr (Wetter?) says these are 33 or 34; it was with some difficulty I coud prevail on Jamison to wait till I had loaded ye Bark. My letter from Provost Fisher obligd me to have the vessel at Bunaw and then advise him: otherwise you may be shure I not waited. I expected also if you had got a freight you woud have advised me sooner.

     Your most affect. Hum: Servtt   John Paterson".

Whatever the cause of this trouble with Archibald Campbell, John Paterson remained on good terms with Coline Campbell. On 17th April

1739 Coline was arranging for Mr Paterson to load a cargo of fir timber ordered by the Strontian company.

In 1740 Mr Paterson proposed a joint company with Coline Campbell to set up a Soap works at "woodend of Kennacraig" and offered to send over from Ireland a man skilled in the trade. The company was to have a capital of £150 and Coline Campbell was to erect a building which was "20 feet within the wall of one gabell". Coline Campbell was expected to buy 20-30,000 lbs of roll tobacco per year from Mr Paterson. Nothing more is known about this proposal.

Two unrelated entries concerning the supply of fir timber from Bonawe to other customers are of interest:

5th Sept 1738 "Given Hugh McLauchlans Ship a fir tree 26 ft long and 33 ins round, ye middle to be a Topmast, the Lightning on Friday last having Broke ye mast". Hugh MacLachlan was the brother of John MacLachlan, the merchant in Fort William, who was a partner in the Oban Company.

The other order was for a cooper. On 13th Sept 1738 "2 fir stocks one 14 ft long & 24 ins round, the oyr 13 ft long & 26 ins round, per Mathew Jack, Couper".

John Baine and Robert Arthur

John Baine, a merchant in Hull, was dealing in spirits, notably ginever from Belgium, and in other "Dutch Goods", especially tea.

On 23rd June 1741, Coline Campbell was debtor to John Baine for the following::

135 pints Ginever at 18d	£10- 2- 6
Rum brandy other spirits	£16- 7
34 pints Ginever	£ 2-11"

Coline was to pay the balance of "£14-17-1 in a month after this at Greenock to Mr Robert Arthur".

A letter dated 28th July 1741 from John Baine in Greenock to Coline Campbell concerns tea. Coline Campbell had bought Scotchon and Imperial canisters and a Congoe chest. Mr Baine asked him to pay Robert Arthur "who advanced me the money, £14-odd. This day I sail for Hull".

Captain Arthur was annoyed with Coline Campbell. On 25th September 1741 he wrote from Crawfordsdyke: "Dear Collin, its strange you have not ordered me payment of your bill you gave baine for what you bought of him and I gave him cash for it he ashuring me you woud order it punctualy at that rate of dowing no body shoud sell any thing in the hylands wt out having such profits as to resolve to be long out of their money. I hope youll order it and the above paytt soon

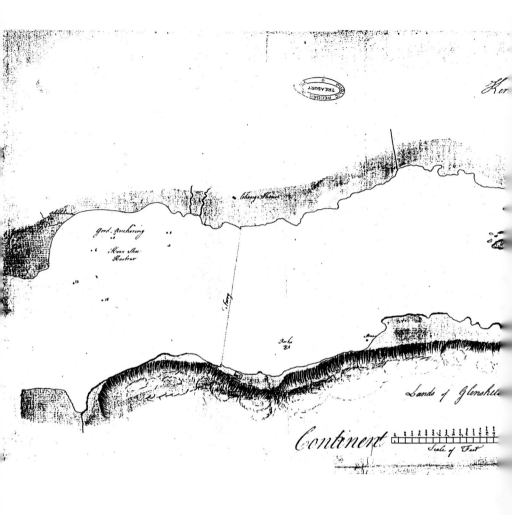

A chart of Oban and the Sound of Kerrera believed to be by Daniel Paterson in 1758. The
words "good anchoring" appear at "Horse shoe Harbour," on the left, behind Heather
Island in the middle, at Oban and at Ardintraive across the bay.
A few scattered buildings are shown at Oban.

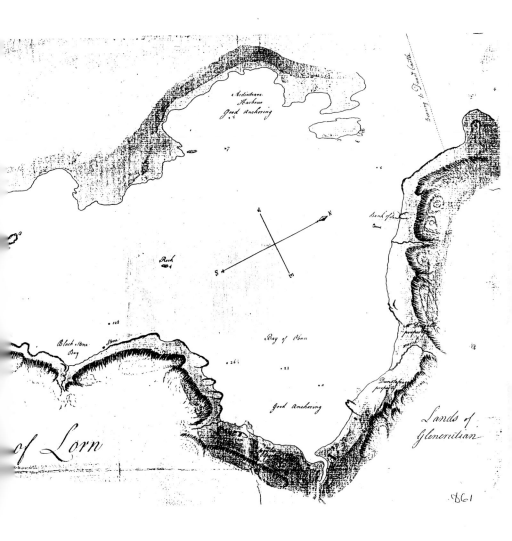

The tobacco mill was built somewhere on the right bank of the stream which marked the
boundary between the Glencruitten Estate of Campbell of Dunstaffnage and the Duke's
Oban Estate of Glenshellach. The MacDougalls of Dunollie, whose Castle projects on the
righthand edge of the Chart, owned the land up to the Tannery Burn, which today flows
below the main road into Oban and exits near the Great Western Hotel.

Is all from   Dr sir   Your Humble Svt   Robt Arthur".

Captain Arthur was losing patience by 8th December 1741 when he again wrote from Crawfordsdyke to Coline Campbell, who was then at Glasgow:
"Dr Sir, Mathew Simson (at Oban) advises me of your paying your bill but Returns the Accott. I want to kno the reasons for by your Letter 8th July you acknolage your Taking Canester 8½ lb and 3 lb out of another this letter I have sent to Campbell and the accott to whom I Expecte youll pay it Now as you and Mr Campbell is togher. I want payment of these two bills for tob soe Long agoo you had paid them to Mr Campbell and Mr Campbell tells me he has the bills still unpaid. Soe to this Desire you and Mr Campbell will give me your ansur In Course so as I may kno hou is to pay me for Depend I will not lay much Longer out of it I have nothing further to add but yt I am
Dr Sir   your Humble Servtt   Robt Arthur".
A bill was enclosed:
"oban 23rd June 1741   £14-17-1
one mònth after pay Robert Arthur Merchant in Crawfordsdyke at the House of John Alexander Writer in Greenock Value Received from John Baine as per accott of this date
accepts   Coline Campbell of Inveresragan   signed John Baine.
(GD 1 / 2 9 / 15)

The *Janet* Shipwrecked off Jura

On 7th April 1742 Robert Arthur of Crawfordsdyke, by now very much his own man, asked Coline Campbell to take a statement from Malcolm Forrest, former Master of the brigantine *Janet* of Greenock, which had been lost off the Small Isles of Jura on 8th February 1742. Mr Arthur wrote "there was Insurance made and the said Forrest having left Greenock before he was Examined as to the circumstances of loss, and is now on board John Watson's Gabert, which I expect is with you or at Fort William. Take his Disposition anent the loss or dispatch an express to George Douglas at Fort William so that he can get it done before any Justice of the peace. If you think the Disposition can be got Expede in a few days, detain the express till you have it returned from Fort William. Pray let it be done as soon as the Gabert appears. Send it by express to Inveraray to be forwarded to me by post and advise your charges".

The circumstances of the shipwreck and rebuttal of any illegality are contained in an undated Disposition by John Lennox, mariner, which was forwarded by Robert Arthur along with a proforma to show how the statement of Malcolm Forrest should be set down. In outline the *Janet* left Sherras(?) about the 4th January 1742 for Stornoway with

12 lasts of barrels and 4 lasts filled with salt. The ship reached Lochramsay, 2 miles from Stornoway, on 9th January, "but the herring fishing was gone". After a fortnight they sailed for Belfast, stayed the next day at the Bishen Isles(?) Then put into Lochdon, (Mull) where they were detained by contrary winds until 7th February. At 8 AM that day they left Lochdon with all sails set and "at midnight the vessel Struck with her Stem upon a blind rock about 4 miles north east of the Small Isles of Jura and was carried by the violence of the tide and wind. She made a vast deal of water, though they plied the pumps constantly until the water was as high as the upper deck, upon which they betook themselves to the boat for the preservation of their lives. They saw her sink entirely ... rowed for twelve hours space and at last got ashore on a little Island called Shuna".

Mr Lennox further stated "that at the time the vessel was lost the foresaid 12 lasts of barrels and the foresaid 4 lasts full of salt were in the same condition as they took them on board, Excepting so much as was made use of in curing five barrels of herring which was all they had on board. This he Depones to be truth as he shall Answer to God".

The owner of the *Janet* was James Leckie of Greenock, but it is clear that Captain Arthur had more than a passing interest in the ship and its cargo.

The *Elise*
Archibald Campbell, formerly manager of the Oban Company, wrote from Glasgow on 13th April 1742 to Coline Campbell: "The *Elise*, Captain Conlon, is to make exportation immediately. Think you should put 10 of your 12 hhds on board and I have ordered as much more of mine as will complete your Certificate, so keep two of the worst of them to spin and let the rest of them go up to Fort William. As soon as the gabert returns ... let them be all shipped on board by Conlon. They will not be above ten days on board of him so youll have them (back) in time enough to answer any other design. This will be clearing the Certificate and keeping John Ritchie from Craiking.
Robine Arthur and I have a great deal of money to pay next week. Pray send me all the cash you possibly can when the gabert goes up. You are by no means to keep any of the tobacco till the gabert has brought it once". This was clearly a planned relanding.

A Shipwreck off Lismore
A letter dated 2nd January 1743 from Donald Campbell of Airds to Coline Campbell reads:
"Dear Colin   Islandnaclach

Friday night a London vessel of 400(?) tons burthen was wrecked here. Her loading was 700 hogsheads tobacco and 90 tons iron. The tobacco is all damaged by salt water and is not yet certain whether the iron is past recovering. I can give no further particulars as I have not seen any of the people on board who last night went for Fyart (Lismore) before I came here. If tobacco in the above situation can be of any use I think you ought to come here.   I am, Yours Donald Campbell".

Another letter to Coline from Airds House, near Appin, later that day reads:

"Dear Inver,

I resolve to come home. I have little to add but that there is three hogsheads put ashore in one of them Islands that has not suffered quite as much as the rest ... I believe you might have them ... it may be worth your while to see it. The iron is gone irrecoverably. This ship occasioned the mistake of its ... lying some time at Lochdon and the tobacco loaded at Dunstaffnage is from the Firth. The transaction at Oban is so villainous that I should be sorry even to suspect any pretending to be a Gentleman of it. Wishing you and yours a happy new year.   I ever am   Dear Inver

yr affect Donald Campbell".

On 14th January 1743 William Cowan of Stirling wrote a rather scornful letter to Coline Campbell from Fort William: "Sir, Just now I received yours acquainting me of a Vessel loaded with tobacco Castaway near Lismore. Some time ago I sent an officer to that place to get a true account. I have by last post acquainted the Commissioners of Same and what directions they gave me I must Govern my Self accordingly. I am informed the tobacco is so much Damaged that its good for nothing but the Gooding of land".

A letter dated 1 February 1743 to Coline Campbell from Humphrey Colquhoun at Maryburgh "in the absence of Mr McVicar" may be relevant to this shipwreck. It reads:

"Capt Cameron was absolved at the Bar as there was no sufficient Witnesses against him. Mr McVicar and others were not examined at all".

Mr Duncan McVicar, who had left the Fort William Excise to become a Merchant in Maryburgh, had some connection with Archibald Campbell, merchant in Oban, formerly manager of the Oban Company. By 1743 Archibald was an independent merchant with offices in Glasgow as well as Oban. . In any event, the reported cargo of 700 hogsheads of tobacco, which would weigh about 200 tons, and the 100 tons of iron, represents a massive increase in the scale of operations in and around Oban, and an enormous loss to the owners of the unnamed ship and its cargo. The tobacco may have been loaded at Dunstaffnage by Oban people, judging by the Airds letter to Coline Campbell, and the loose business connection known to be between Archibald Campbell and Duncan McVicar. Islandnacloich, which is within sight of Oban, is one of the very small islands not far from Achnacroish off the east coast of Lismore. Perhaps the wreck still lies there unrecorded!

Trade with the Isle of Man

Many merchants and prominent smugglers were admitted as burgesses when visiting Inveraray. They included John Somervell of Renfrew (1727), John Hyndman in Greenock (1728), John Paterson in Glasgow (1730), John Richardson, clerk at Strontian (1735), Archibald Campbell in Glasgow, almost certainly the Oban manager (1736) and James Christie in Stirling (1736). There is no record of Bailie John Steuart of Inverness, who is known to have had Jacobite sympathies.
            (Burgesses of Inveraray)
James Duke of Atholl, Lord of Man and the Isles and many of his large retinue were admitted as burgesses of Inveraray on 17th September 1744. Atholl owned the Isle of Man, which had for long been the entrepot for smuggling by merchants in the Lowlands and in England. Their story has been fully documented by Frances Wilkins. (Wilkins)

There are very few references to the Isle of Man in the Inveresragan records. The Lowland and Glasgow merchants may have discouraged direct trade between the Highlands and the Isle of Man to protect their established agents. The Articles of the first Oban Company giving its proposed scope specifically stated "Isle of Man excepted".

Not until the end of 1741 do we find Coline Campbell and Archibald Campbell, the Oban merchant, combining to trade with the Island. On 29th December the accounts show that they bought 1000 gallons of rum costing £141-13s-4d from Robert & James Berrie, to be delivered by Messrs Ross and Black of Douglas.
John Campbell, the Oban-based skipper of the schooner *Nancy* of Colonsay, who may have been on a second journey to the Isle of Man, left Oban on 11th March 1742 and returned to "the horse shoe" on 17th April. Rather belatedly Archibald Campbell wrote from Glasgow to Coline on 17th March; "I wrote you about the schooner last night but forgot to tell you to take in all Mr Richardsons seed lying at Oban and he is to deliver it to Messrs Ross and Black in the Isle. I mean he is to take on board as much as he handsomely can, not to overload himself".

John Campbell's expenses for this voyage, invoiced to Archibald &

Coline Campbell, totalled £4-18-10d and included:

A pilot from Peel to Douglas   5 shillings
Porterage to load the cargo
Beef, salt herring and meal for the crew
Ale for their porrige, 4 pints
Pecks of meal in Barnashalaig
Milk and eggs in Easdale
Finlay Gray's wages for 1 month and ten days   17 shillings
John Mcpherson's wages at 9 shillings per month   13 shillings
Express to Mr McVicar when going to Island
Giving out 4 bottles of whisky   4 shillings

David Ross and Robert Black wrote from Douglas to Coline in March 1742:

"Yours of 18th current by John Campbell, we have delivered 1000 gallons of rum. The hatches of Mr Campbell's vessel would not take in large pieces but we gave him as many as we could and were obliged to furnish him with small casks to make up the quantity which he assured us you would thankfully pay for. Have sent you 2 hhds wine at £7 per hhd and 2 ankers Shrub. All amounts to £22-4s for which I have drawn on you payment in three months to the order of Mr Thomas Wallace, which with Mr James Campbell's draught on you and Mr Archd Campbell in our favour for £16-4-3d we do not doubt you will duly honour".

On his return skipper John Campbell wrote to Coline from "the horse shoe" on Sunday 18th April 1742: "I came from the Island yesterday, was eight days, but had mostly contrary winds and calm weather. Immediately desire to know whats to be done with the cargo and be no longer under (my) concern for it. It is contained in large Casks and I assure you it was no less than Great Bargain to have it so because they are the weakest and silliest ever I saw. Had I money to buy small casks I would have done it. If good care be not taken you may lose the value of a hundred casks. I was obliged to draw into small casks 300 gallons of it because our hatch would not receive large puncheons.
I took from Mr Ross 2 hogsheads of new Claret & 2 ankers of shrub for you, you'll receive along with this from Messrs Ross and Black. I believe the shrub can be sold for six shillings per gallon.
Your humble servant   John Campbell".

John Campbell listed the cargo as "31 ankers & 11 terses and a hogshead rum", as well as the 2 hogsheads wine and 2 ankers of shrub mentioned above. Judging by his letter this well-documented voyage was contraband and it wasn't until 5th May that Coline Campbell sent an express to notify Fort William Custom House about the cargo. In August he noted expenses for rum sold on Mull, for a visit to Tyndrum on 15th May to sell rum with Achallader, to making twelve 25-pint ankers for the rum and to the hire of 10½ horses at 8s per horse to take rum to Monteith. Clearly this surfeit of rum had not been fully declared at the Customs House!

There was another trade in 1742 detailed in a letter from Douglas signed by David Ross and Robert Black to Coline Campbell dated 10th September:
"Yours of 20th ult by Mr Stewart. Have delivered for your accott 5 hhds claret, 1 hhd white wine and 2 casks Shrub amounting (below) to £46-14-10d to the order of Mr Thomas Wallace junior in Glasgow. I think No 2 will be soonest fit for use so you may bottle it first. Youll find all these wines to your contentment as they are the best and cheapest of their kind. Your last wine was just a little green. Mr Stewart had a letter of credit to Mr Forbes from whom he took his wine. We shall desire Mr Wallace to take your payments." The details of the order were:

3 hhds claret No 1 at £6-10s per hhd	£19-10s
1 hhd No 2	£ 7
1 hhd No 3	£ 8-10s
1 hhd best french white wine	£ 5-10s
2 ankers, 20 gallons, Shrub at 6s per gallon	£ 6
porterage etc	4s- 10d
total	£46-14s 10d

There follows helpful suggestions on how to "force white wine" as follows:
"Add the whites of 15 eggs beaten to a froth with a handful of coarse salt to 5 or 6 gallons of wine drawn off. Then put this back in the hogshead and work it well with a forcing brush or a pretty large stick cloven in four for 6 to 8 minutes. It will be fine in about 15 days and you may bottle it in clear weather". A postscript adds "You may follow the same directions to force your white wine only take half a handful of salt and half a handful of fine sand instead of the eggs".

Coline sent a letter dated 27th April 1743 to Messrs Ross and Black in Douglas, by the hand of Archibald Orr, master of the *James* of Inverkip. The letter with the order was signed by Coline Campbell and Archibald Buchanan, merchant in Oban and reads "you are to send in such packages or casks as to be liable to no seizures, should the Vessel be forced in on either side of the channel. But let the casks be of the smallest size the Law directs. The Clearance is to be made out for Norway".
Coline's instruction to Mr Orr of the same date, before he sailed, reads.
"You are hereby ordered to sail with the first fair wind from Oban for

Douglas in the Isle of Man and there bring on board Two tons of wine and three tons and a half brandy spirits to be received of Messrs Ross and Black and hence to sail with all dispatch for the Sound of Kerrera. Then deliver us the Said cargo for which run we oblige us to pay you on Delivery ten pounds sterling".

Archibald Orr returned empty-handed on 13th May.
Robert Black's reply to Coline Campbell and Archibald Buchanan reads:
"Gentlemen, Yours of 27th April by Mr Archibald Orr to Mr Ross and me came duly to hand and I notice your commission ... which I am sorry to acquaint you it is not now in my power to answer. I have no acquaintance with either of you and Mr Ross is just now in your Country and I act here for him as well as for myself. What makes me Cautious of giving Credit to any one whose character and circumstances I am not very well acquainted with and what makes me still more scrupulous is to find that the goods that were sent to Mr Campbell 8 months ago are not yet quite paid for. As you'll probably see Mr Ross e'er he leaves Scotland, if you'll get leave from him your commission shall be punctually observed. (signed) Robert Black".

On 13th May Archibald Buchanan wrote from Oban to Coline: "Mr Orr arrived here this evening with Mr Black's reply and is anxious to be away for Clyde". Unsuccessful attempts were then made to contact Mr Ross. Matthew Simson, by now probably working for Archibald Campbell, the former manager at Oban, wrote from Glasgow to Coline Campbell on 28th May: "Mr Campbell desires to advise you that Mr Ross from the Isle of Man was gone before your letter came to hand". On June 15th Archibald Campbell himself wrote from Glasgow to Coline about an outstanding earlier debt to Ross and Black "So soon as you can bring with you the accounts of the rum and tobacco so as we may settle them. Pray remit me without loss of time ... it has been hard upon me to pay back the tobacco and rum".

David Ross wrote to Coline Campbell from Douglas on 20th August 1743:
"Sir, I understand you wrote to this house in my absence for a large parcel of goods and sent a Vessel for them. If I had been at home I would not have let her go away without her cargo. Mr Black had no advice of the former bills being paid and we are often disappointed in payments in your country ... besides we know nothing about Archibald Buchanan who signed with you. As you are so well acquainted in Glasgow you may easily get a friend there whom we know to sign orders with you. In that case you may have what goods you please of all kinds and at as low prices as if you was to pay ready money for them. I dare say you are a man of so good sense as not to

take this precaution of ours amiss as we daily meet with rubs which put us on our guard. We would willingly serve you both in price and quality as well as any in the Island, especially in Wines. We have lately got a large parcel of Canary and dry mountain wines both very good of their kinds and will be sold reasonable; and they are wines not to be had anywhere else at this time. I am Sir, Your most humble servt, David Ross",

The only other surviving letter about trade with the Isle of Man was a curt note from Thomas Wallace, Merchant in Glasgow, who had signed a previous order with Coline Campbell. He wrote to Coline on 22nd February 1743: "I know nothing as to the price of wines, etc, in the Isle of Man". Messrs Ross and Black had trusted Coline Campbell when Mr Wallace signed earlier orders with him, but he was no longer willing to vouch for Coline

The End at Oban and Inveresragan
During 1742 what remained of the Oban Company was being run down. For example,
on 14th September a note from Coline Campbell requested Archibald Buchanan at Oban to fill four casks with rum "from the Broached rum cask at Oban". On 15th September Archibald Buchanan sent "order with bearer, total 100 pints".

Between 1743 and 1745 the individuals at Oban were operating only on a small scale
Coline Campbell kept an unsigned copy in his own hand of two letters he wrote on 11 February 1743. He wrote, presumably to the Company:
"Gentlemen,
I do not in the least doubt of the straits you are in for money which ever must be the case if the way things are carried on at Disolving the compy as soon after the profit & loss should be known. this we all know was not the case, nor is it to this day nor am afraid ever will be the case considering how subjects were confounded. Its right every one should advance what he is justly obliged to, and it is as just the compy should acct to me for what they got: but to sign & corrobarat Deeds without knowing how matters stand after being Struck out of your Company several years ago its what I think cannot with any justice be defended and is what I will not agree to until a fair Slate is made. And should the company use harsh methods the Law is potent ... but this method I do not choose ... let us see how we stand and none will be readier to contribute his Share than I. For this purpose once more appoint a proper place for all to meet and give it the finishing Stroke. This is the only way to prevent further confusion ...

if you judge this a right method let me know in time and receive your paper.

I am gentlemen, your most humble servant   Inver 11 febry 1743".
(unsigned copy).

On the same day Coline wrote to Archibald Campbell:
"Dear Archd,

I wrote you with regard to your nephew John in a particular manner. I had a letter from the company about ye concern with a paper to sign which I cannot conceive the use ... were I to do things again I know not if I'd sign as many as I have   For God's sake lett things be brought to some place or oyr. Is it prudent for rational people to act in this way that is done since ye Dissolution of our Company ... can it be Imagined that people who are Struck out of a Company are still to be supposed to be in it and to be concerned in the subsequent transactions ... let the members of that old Company once meet with a full Resolution to end all in such a way as people of business should do.   Until I see some probability of this I Declare I'll Decline doing anything come what will: I have wrote them to this purpose by which I resolve to stand. I have been Idle enough to spend my tyme and money at meetings to no purpose ... if they will meet it must be at oban or near it. Besides the march season is just at hand that will not admitt to my being long or far from home.

I know not a case lyes so heavy on me as this unlucky affair. Let something to purpose be done ... but I will insist that things must come to a close.   I am afraid I have worried you but I cannot help it, the state of Rum & Tobacco sent to Perthshire as you have Inclosed. I hope by my next to be in a condition to make you a remittance only advise me how you stand as to the Barrys. Ritchy keeps him in a right way and let me know what you are in advance for him which I'll remitt directly ... and I am

　　　　　Dr Archd　　　your affectionate　　　(unsigned copy)

In May 1743 it was planned to disperse the remaining stocks at Oban

An unsigned copy letter written by Archibald Campbell in Glasgow was sent to Coline at Inveresragan and reads:
"Receive a letter to Airds with a bill to sign of £130 ... and he will get up the bill of £201-13-4 this send the minute you get to oban and send me the bill signed for £150

tell archie Buchanan to send everything that comes home by John Bane (Baine) or by Hugh McLachlane (John MacLachlan's brother) that is sensible and moveable away from oban viz powder and tea ... to send them to some safe houses up amongst the Tennants privatlie at some distance and let the powder be sent to the Baillie Montearans and the tea spread up and doun and sent to my mothers and the

Barron Duncross as fast as possible and particularlie that which belongs to myself ... and let him (Buchanan) take care that John Banes being there does not make a noise and bring doun the Custom house. When Hugh McLachlane comes see every thing be Cautiouslie manadged. Pray see to gather in money as fast as possiblie you can and see to get Donald and Johnie pleased with their uncle". (Is this a coded message?)

On 29th August 1743 Archibald Campbell was owed a total of £202-19 by Coline Campbell, who had apparently withdrawn from the Oban Company on 26th September 1740. (GD 1 / 2 2/4).
In 1743 the whole Oban company debts were £1,630. Mr Fogo wrote: "The heads have accepted half and each partner is to pay £100 on account".

On 3rd January 1744 John MacLachlan owed the Oban Company £400, mostly for wines and spirits, including rum from the West Indies. A letter sent on 19th February 1744 by William Fogo, David Young and Archibald Campbell to John MacLachlan and Coline Campbell informed them that the bills of John and Coline had not been accepted by "the heads".
However the Inveresragan tobacco mill was still in operation in 1744 because 12 hogsheads of leaf, brought up in two boats from Matthew Simson's gabbart in Oban in December 1743, were rolled at Inveresragan between January and October 1744

Two 1744 letters from Robert Arthur were aimed at selling leaf tobacco he had stored at Oban. The first, to James Fisher, Merchant at Inveraray, was written at Taynish on 21st July and reads: "I have left 10 hogsheads at Oban, which will do very well for roll. I shall be glad to serve you with five of the best. If you please send your tobacco spinner to look at them you may have any of them at 5d (payable in) six or nine months time. I shall wait to hear if you take them because I can sell them otherwise". (GD 1 / 2 15/141)
On 5th October he wrote from Crawfordsdyke to Coline Campbell: "I expected you would have taken a look at the tobacco at Oban before now. You have really hindered me to sell it otherwise. I have only seen A. C. once since I saw you at Dumbarton. He is playing the fool with himself and will expose himself".

A third Robert Arthur letter was written from Glasgow to Coline Campbell on 25th October 1744 about the debts and reads: "I was much surprised at your refusal. Mr Campbell is upon the bond 1737 where there is a balance of £500. John MacLachlan is upon the bond 1738 where this is only £200 odd. This submission is not only to raise money to pay this demand but also all other demands. Its very ungenerous your refusing to meet when Mr Campbell is distressed for your bond when he has no manner of concern. Besides days ago Wm Fogo was so bad his life was despaired of. He is not yet a great deal better. You know what terrible confusion his death would put us into ... so for god sake come so as we may get something done when in life".

(GD 1 / 2 15/166)

On the same day, 25th October 1744, the following letter to Coline Campbell was signed by Archibald Campbell, Robert Arthur and John MacLachlan.

"Sir, we are very much surprised ... you mistake your not being concerned in the bonds which are distressed ... near £500 many by the old company and the latest 1738 for £200. Mr Fogo has been very ill and you know what hard consequences it would be if not done before anything was to happen to him". (GD 1 / 2 15/166)

On 4th December 1744 Archibald Campbell in Glasgow wrote to Coline Campbell:

"the old company debts are to be paid equally by us, John McLachlan David Young Robert Arthur Archibald Campbell William & Henry Fogo ... we are fully determined to prosecute you and Collonsa ... and Diligence is our only way.

(signed)   Archd Campbell   John MacLachlan

The debts were stated to be "upwards of £3000, 2/3rds of which affect the old Company".

Duncan McVicar at Maryburgh sounded a warning to Coline Campbell on 26th December 1744: "I have been with the Sheriff of Inverness. A *Surefacius* is against John MacLachlan, Archibald Campbell and you. The Sheriff was particularly inclined against you. The sum claimed exceeded £1,100 Sterling. I wish to God you may soon get yourself disengaged of that company affair". (GD 1 / 2 15/181)

From 1745 onwards letters and accounts are fragmentary. It can be concluded that the Fogo brothers, David Young & other merchants had no further contact with Inveresragan. The last significant letter was one from Robert Arthur to Coline Campbell on 7th May 1745 to say that the whole company debt was £3,200.

The shop at Inveresragan closed between 27th May and 5th June 1745 and one can be fairly sure that Coline died at the end of May. His brother Archibald in Inveraray and his son James both ordered black material for funeral clothing from the Inveresragan shop just before 27th May. The shop reopened, but records ceased before the end of 1745.

The correspondence and records of Inveresragan effectively ended with Coline's death.

Coline left the problems and debts to his son James. There is no sign that the debts were ever repaid unless it was through the sale of the Inveresragan lands (to Ardchattan).

Letters to James in the files up to 1747, are very few in number, and sometimes concerned trivial amounts. For example:

On 5th March 1747 John Campbell, Writer in Inveraray, sent James a note of money owed by "the Deceast Colin Campbell of Inveresragan for expenses due in Scots money to Donald Kennedy, Sheriff officer" namely:

"June 1738 poynding with 3 men for 17 days at 6d per day

£15- 6 Scots

To his own trouble   £10-16 Scots

Decmbr 1738   Charging & Summonding through Lorn

Lismore, Appin Lochaber & Glencow   £10-14 Scots"

On 10th February 1748, £27-1-2½ Sterling was owed to Alexander Campbell and Arthur Connell, merchants in Glasgow, by "Successors of Coline Campbell of Inveresragan".

On 26th August 1747 James Campbell Esq of Inveresragan was admitted a burgess of Inveraray as "Ensign in Inverawe's Company".

(Burgesses of Inveraray)

James may have served during the Jacobite Rebellion of 1745-46. Reading between the lines his earlier youthful attempts to become a man of business had been less than successful and the military life may have suited him better.

There was a complete but brief interruption in trading activities during the Jacobite Rebellion before normal business was resumed.

Archibald Campbell who had moved to Glasgow, almost certainly was the Campbell in the partnership of Fogo & Campbell, which was recorded between 1748 and 1752.

In April 1748, Wm Fogo and Archd Campbell purchased tobacco from Andrew & Ard Buchanan. This could have been Archibald Buchanan, formerly clerk of the Oban Company.

And on 20th August 1752, Wm Fogo and Archd Campbell were in a transaction with James Baird junior.

(Dell SRO B 10/12/1 folio 180-181)

It is known that the Fogo brothers were still importing tobacco during the 1750s

On 14th February 1743 Robert Arthur & Co, described as tobacco importers, were associated with Archibald Campbell, Merchant in Glasgow, Robert Russell and George Douglas, Merchant in

Maryburgh. (Dell SRO TD 89/1)
In his long career, Robert Arthur went on to become one of the leading shipowners and merchants in Western Scotland from a base at Irvine, which he moved to in 1760. (Cullen)

Fort William with the village of Maryburgh in the foreground. Artist believed to be Paul Sandby, c. 1747. Reproduced with permission of the West Highland Museum, Fort William.

Dunstaffnage Bay and Castle by an unknown artist. Smuggled cargoes were sometimes transferred here into smaller boats for relanding at Inveresragan in Loch Etive. Reproduced with permission of Madam Morag MacDougall of Dunollie.

The Firth of Lorn and the mountains of Mull, seen from near Oban.

Bonawe Harbour on the North shore of Loch Etive as it is today. Smuggled goods were probably put ashore here or at Inveresragan, although the main part of the village was on the South shore. Ben Cruachan is in the background.

Looking eastward from Inveresragan towards Bonawe and Ben Cruachan. The shore here was some way from Coline Campbell's shop and tobacco mill, the remains of which lie around today's farm steading.

"The horse shoe", Horseshoe Bay on Kerrera Island. This anchorage was most favoured for smuggling, being out of sight of prying eyes in Oban village.

All that remains today of the iron furnace at Glenkinglas, on the remote north-eastern shore of Loch Etive.

Oban Bay and the Village of Oban (around 1760-70) by Lieut John Pierie RN. The view is looking North past Dunollie Castle to Lismore and Morvern. Reproduced with permission of the National Maritime Museum, Greenwich.

APPENDIX A
THE LOCHETTY COMPANY & THE OBAN COMPANIES
The Lochetty Company: 1728-1733

The partnership called the Lochetty Company was formed on 15th May 1728 by Coline Campbell of Inveresragan, Duncan Campbell of Inverawe, John Campbell of Lossit and John Campbell of Barcaldine. Barcaldine was bought out in 1730 by William Fogo of Kilhorn. The partnership ended on 26th April 1733, and formally on 27th July that year, and the accounts were finalised at a meeting at Fernoch, near Taynuilt, on 29th May 1736

Coline Campbell's shop at Inveresragan served the whole area of Lorn and the shop day-books are fascinating and detailed, but outside the scope of this publication.

The Oban Companies: From 1735

The Oban Company was formed at a meeting in Glasgow on 30th December 1734.

The Minutes of formal meetings of the Oban Company are recorded twice in date order in the Archives at Ardchattan The two copies have been compared and, though of different lengths because of the size of handwriting, were found to be almost identical.

The copy in a soft brown cover has the following words in Coline Campbell's hand on the cover:

(GD 1/2/17/ 7/1-7/5)

"This side of this book contains a coppy of the Acts of Sederunt of the Oban Company till 11th May 1739 and the State of Said Company with regard to the Capitals advanced then & now till Joind by John McLachlan & Colonsay in February 1736".

The other side of the book contains copies of letters sent by Coline Campbell as Manager of the Lochetty Company, from February 1730 to May 1732.   (GD 1/2/15/206)

The six-page contract of the first Oban company, drawn up in Glasgow, has only been seen in a draft copy, which is difficult to read. The contract on 30th December 1734 is between:

"On the one part   Daniell Mcneill, Yr of Colonsa for Malcom
                                 Mcneill, his father Neill Campbell of Achinard
                                 David Young, Merchant in Glasgow
                  and   William Somervell, Writer there
& on the other part   William & Henry Fogo and Archibald Gray,
                                 Merchants in Glasgow".

The parties to earlier contracts had been:
Malcom Mcneill, Neill Campbell & William Somervell on 7th September 1733.
And William Somervell & David Young on 28th December 1733.

The draft Oban contract reads in part as follows:
"Malcom Mcneill, Neill Campbell and William Sommerveill, being resolved to carry on in Company a manufactory of tobacco, cause work the Sclate Craigs and quarries in the Island of Kerula or any other part of the Laird of McDougalls Estate.   And such other

branches of trade as to them should seem convenient. And for that purpose they had taken a tack of the Land of Glencruttan more from Angus Campbell of Dunstaffnage, and intended to build a House at oban which is part of the Sd Lands for Manufactory." (each paid in) "one hundred pounds Sterling as a stock for Carrying out in Company in building the forsd House, procuring the forsd Tack, purchasing Tools for the Slate quarries, paying the price of the forsd seven hundred and fifty three bolls Meall.

"The sd David Young and William Sommerveill have made offer to each of the sd William and Henry Fogo and Archibald Gray of an equal share with each person of the forsd Company (as partners) and of their shop goods at oban of £158 Sterling purchased by David Young on the credit of the oban company".

At the beginning "Collonsa" (Malcom McNeill of Colonsay) was a sleeping partner.

Neill Campbell of Achinard, a partner in the separate Meal Company, was involved in 1733 in the import of the753 bolls of meal mentioned in the draft contract. There was no record of the disposal of this purchase, which was to pose financial problems later.

APPENDIX B – SHIPS TRADING IN OBAN AREA 1725-1745

Ship	Master	year
Agnes of Glasgow (bark)	Archibald Stewart	1724 & 26
Hereward	Edward Nixon	1729
Robert Ramsay	(John Somervell connection)	1729
Sea Flower of Creills	Andrew Breudie	1730
Margareen	Richard Kelsick	1731
Thomas of Maryburgh	John Gibson (export to Ireland)	1731
Providence of Gourock	Wm Hasty & 3 crew (22 tons)	1731
Diamond	Robert Arthur of Crawfords Dyke	1730-43
Agnes gabbart	Capt Cockel	1731
	James Beaton	1733-34
Mary & Jean of Gourock	George Dennie, Master	1730
Mary & Jean of Gourock	Jeremiah Campbell	1732
Mary & Jean of Gourock	John McNeil, Master	1733
James of Gourock	John McCun of Gourock (brig 40 tons)	1733
Jean of Irvine	John Miller	1732-34
Diligence of Irvine	Robert King	1732/4/5/6
Alexander of Saltcoats		1730s
Margaret of Weems	George Thomson	1738 & 43
Ann of Scalaster		1730s
Betty	Daniel McLeish (seized Tobermory)	1732
Strontian (sloop)	Duncan Fletcher (seized Tobermory)	1732
Nathaniel & John of Derry	John Henderson (seized Dunstaffnage)	1732
Robert & Ralph of Newcastle	John Skinner in Greenock	1733 & 36
Sally		1736
Agnes of Port Glasgow (brig)	David Beaton	1736

Lyon of Irvine		1736
Providence		1736
Recovery of Fort William		1736
Nancy	Mr Glass	1730s
William & John of Irvine		1737
Janett of Inverkip	Archibald Orr (good ship 22 tons)	1734
Friendship of Saltcoats	Robert Barber	1734
Glasgow pacquet of		
Greenock	John Hyndman	
	of Greenock (owner)	1734
	Robert Sinclair (brig)	
Black Bitch of Elphinstone	William Hodge (seized at Airth)	1733-36
Peggy of Achindown		1737 & 38
Bettie		1740
Nancy of Colonsay	John Campbell,	
	Shipmaster Oban	1741-43
Jannet of Greenock (brig)	Malcolm Forrest	
	(shipwrecked off Jura)	1742
Elise	Capt Conlon	1742
"London Vessel" (400 tons)	Capt Cameron/Mr McVicar?	
	(shipwrecked)	1743
Dove	Andrew Broun	1744

Links to unnamed vessels and boats

	Captain Angus Campbell	1728
	Mr Drummond's ship (at Appin)	1731
	John Mcneill in Port Glasgow	1733
	Daniel McNeil	
	(mercht in Machrahanish)	1732
	Robert Haxton,	
	shipmaster in Burntisland	1733
	John Smith, Skipper of Belfast	1737-38
	Mr Daniel Shiel(d)s of Baneranoch	1737
	Robert Hunter, shipmaster in Irvine	
	John Broun (see Andrew Broun, above)	
	George Dennie	
	Robert Morrison's boat	1740
	Alexr roy Campbell, boatman in	
	Lagavullin In Islay	1744

Local ships & boats

	Donald McAndra(ew) boatman	
	at Bonawe	1732-40
	(Actual name Donald Macfarlane)	
	Nicol McNiven, ferrier at Bonawe	1742-45
	Conallys sloop	1737
	Alexander Browne's boat	1735
	John Ferguson,	
	shipmaster (at Connel)	1738
	John Campbells boat	
	(at Oban, see above)	1736-44

John Mcphaden, skipper
John McInnes in Port Kerrera 1737
Hugh McLachlans ship (at Bonawe) 1738
William Park's boat (at Bonawe) 1740
Matthew Simson,
sailor in Gourock 1743
John McEinrioch,
ferrier at Rownacarn. 1742

APPENDIX C – BACKGROUND INTEREST
Postal Service at Inveraray
The postal (and innkeeping!) accounts of Archibald Campbell, brother
of Coline Campbell of Inveresragan contain a wealth of detail,
especially GD 1 / 2 11/3.
The relevant references are:

GD 1 / 2 11/3	Account book belonging to Archibald Campbell, Inveraray
GD 1 / 2 11/4	1734 postal accounts to and from Inveraray. This includes many letters to & from Collector John MacNeill and some sent onwards as far as Campbeltown.
GD 1 / 2 11/5	1735 postal account for whole year.
GD 1 / 2 11/6	Postage account from 1742 to last entry 24 June 1745 Includes 1739 account for tobacco and customs account for 1739
GD 1 / 2 11/7	Miscellaneous accounts for tea, rum, claret & debts paid by January 1740.

A letter to or from Glasgow cost twopence (2d), to or from Edinburgh
4d, while packages over six ounces cost double and those over ten
ounces could cost as much as 10d, 1s/4d or 2s/2d Nearly all letters
were paid for on collection by the recipient.
Some monthly totals are:

	Mar 35	Apr 35	Dec 35	Jan 36	Feb 36	Mar 36	Apr 36	May 36
Rec.	19s/4d	30s/4d	24s/4d	13s/4d	12s/4d	24s/4d	55s/6d	10s/4d
Sent	28s/4d	34s/4d	41s/8d	36s/4d	30s/4d	26s/4d	67s/8d	31s/4d

The names of all the senders and receivers are recorded.

Archibald was the leading innkeeper in Inveraray, hosting social
events. For example:
On 10th October 1735, he claimed "£2-10s for 24 bottles of claret and
a chopin of brandy at the Election of the Magistrates". And on 16th
January 1736 he claimed 5 shillings for 3 bottles of white wine and 6
ounces of sugar consumed by "the Magistrates and Toun Council".
One of the few early mentions of whisky is dated 4th December 1733
when Archibald "bought a cask of whisque from Mr McAlister at
tarbart for 10 shillings a gallon".
Archibald only once bought tobacco from his brother at Inveresragan,
claiming that he could buy it in Inveraray at the same price as at
Bonawe. Besides the Inveraray innkeepers "were thirled to their local

merchants".

Staff and Workers at the Glenkinglas furnace
The shop daybooks at Inveresragan contain the names of managers
and purchases made on behalf of named workers. The latest
recorded date is 1741.
Rodger Murphy, Manager at the furnace
Charles Coyle, Manager   do
Duncan McNab (Manager?)   do
Malcolm McNab, smith   do
John Maguire   do
Duncan McMillan   do
John Whett   do
Mr Allan   do
Donald og McLehonnel   do
John Swan, weaver at the furnace   (GD 1/2/14 12/9 of 3/10/1741
                                   (& GD ref 7/4 of 22/8/1738)
Ann Crawford at Glenkinglas
Shop purchases were made at Inveresragan for the following named
persons "at the furnace"

Terlach Mcquaran	Gilly Gerum	Michell Brittain
John Byrne	James Doyle	William Carroll & his wife
James Lochan	Hugh Ferrall	Edward Mash (verified)
Patrick Murray	William Mitchell	Ferral Rork

Donald Campbell of Airds
As well as the episode of the shipwreck off Lismore, Donald
Campbell of Airds features several times in the correspondence as a
friend of Coline Campbell. For example:
A letter from Donald Campbell warns Coline Campbell: "The
gentleman who repairs the Barracks is to pursue you for not sending
the timber for the pallisades in terms of your agreement with Mr
Muir". (Surveyor of Customs at Fort William)   (GD 1 / 2 9/7)

There is a letter from Francis Place, Clerk at Strontian lead mines to
Coline Campbell, dated 23rd September 1733 about Donald
Campbell of Airds.
"Respected Friend,
The Stile thou writes in is very merry and agreeable enough to a
mind at Ease.
Thou canst be of great Service to the Company since my old friend
and Acquaintance Donald Campbell has laid an embargo on a great
quantity of Our Lead. Which he Vainly attempted to carry away last
Munday by force. Therefore ... oblige the Company to come to this
place.
I am with great truth thy Sincere Friend Francis Place" (GD 1 / 2 9/7)

Notable Burgesses of Inveraray
Visitors to Inveraray were often admitted as Burgesses as well as
prominent residents,
The following admissions are of interest to the smuggling story. The
names come from "Burgesses of Inveraray" (See References below).

17/07/24	Malcolm McNeill of Colonsay
1724	John Brown, tobacco spinner in Inveraray
05/10/25	Philip Innes, tobacco spinner in Inveraray
07/08/27	James Simson, Ships Master in Crawfords Dyke
05/12/27	John Somervell, Bailie and Merchant in Renfrew
08/07/28	John Hyndman, Merchant in Greenock
06/06/29	John McDugald of Dunollie (Pardoned 1727)
29/09/29	James Woodrow, Collector of Excise in Argyllshire
17/06/30	John Paterson, Merchant in Glasgow
25/09/30	John Campbell, Writer in Inveraray, servant to Archd Campbell, Sheriff Clerk of Argyle.
23/05/31	Adam Fisher, son to James Fisher, late Provost of Inveraray
09/12/31	Captain Arthur Galbraith of the City of Dublin.
09/12/31	Archibald Campbell, brother to Coline Campbell of Inveresragan
30/03/32	George Bogle, Merchant in Glasgow & ptnr in the rope works at Gourock
22/09/35	Mr John Richardson, Clerk at Strontian
10/10/35	Mr James Stevenson, minister at Ardchattan
17/02/36	Mr Archd Campbell, merchant in Glasgow (Manager at Oban?)
19/04/36	James Christie, merchant in Stirling
10/10/41	Angus Fisher, Postmaster in Inveraray
22/06/45	Major William Caulfield, Lieut Governor of Fort Augustus
22/06/45	Mr Robert Bogle of Glasgow, Merchant
26/08/47	Archibald Campbell of Glenshellich (the Duke's Oban Estate).
26/08/47	James Campbell of Inveresragan, Ensign in Inverawe's Company

APPENDIX D
THE INVERESRAGAN RECORDS AT ARDCHATTAN PRIORY

This narrative was compiled largely from eleven boxes of letters and accounts held in the archives of Ardchattan Priory. All but one concern Coline Campbell of Inveresragan.

GD 1 / 2 1-2/ 1-4	Account books , local trade
GD 1 / 2 5/ –7-7	including bound account books as follows:
6/1	"Waste Book" Expenses incurred by Coline Campbell of Inveresragan from June 1728 to 11 May 1733
7/1 - 7/9	Shop day books at Inveresragan 16 Dec 1734 - 29 Nov 1745
GD 1 / 2 8-11	Account books, local trade
GD 1 / 2 12/1 – 13/4	Account books for Inveresragan
GD 1 / 2 14/1 – 14/18	Ardchattan Ledgers and Waste Books – NOT Inveresragan (See "Historic Argyll" reference, in Appendix E, below)
GD 1/ 2 15 1-205	Individual letters mounted in two blue books,

1733-45
206   Letter-book of Coline Campbell in his own hand
       1731-32
       Oban Company acts of sederunt, Dec 1734 -May
       1739
       Stock in trade of first Oban Company
GD 1 / 2 17 1–2/1 Letters to Coline 1725-1733, mostly 32 & 33
       (bundles)
GD 1 / 2 17 2/2-2/4 Mostly invoices & accounts 1726-44 (bundles)
GD 1 / 2 17 2/5 – 2/8 Letters to Coline Campbell of Inveresragan by
       Wm Fogo et al
GD 1 / 2 17 9/1 – 9/16 Letters to Coline 1726-1742 ('42 large bundle)
       +1743 & 44
GD 1 / 2 17 9/19 – 10/5 Letters to Coline. 10/1 to 10/5 (1730-34) & 9/17
       to 18 (43-44)
GD 1 / 2 17 10/6 –12 Letters to Coline (bundles)
Note
The bound books are inscribed: "SRO 16 Aug 1957, Binding &
Repair Section".
All documents in the six boxes designated "17" are loosely bundled
by year. The letters are mostly legible but some were too delicate to
unfold and dust was a hazard. It would be difficult for another
researcher to find the correct box for any manuscript which is
bundled. Where the year is known, it would be necessary to search
several of the "Number 17" boxes (above) for the bundle of that year.

APPENDIX E REFERENCES & SOURCES CONSULTED
References

(RCAHMS) Argyll Volume 2 Lorn. Published by the Royal
Commission on the Ancient and Historical Monuments of Scotland,
1975.
(WORMELL) The Pine Woods of Blackmount by Peter Wormell:
Dalesman Publishing Company, Stable Courtyards, Broughton Hall,
Skipton, N. Yorkshire BD23 3AJ.
(GIBSON) Ships of the '45 by John S Gibson. Hutchinson & Co,
London W1, 1967
(BURGESSES OF INVERARAY) The Burgesses of Inveraray 1665-
1963. Elizabeth Beaton and Sheila W Macintyre (Eds). SRS New
Series 14 Edinburgh 1990.
(HISTORIC ARGYLL) Early Trading from Ardchattan 1743-46 by
Charles Hunter Journal of Lorn Archaeological &Historical Society,
No 8, 2003 pp 19-24 (c. £2.50).
(STEUART LETTERBOOK) Introduction to the Letterbook of Bailie
John Steuart of Inverness, 1715-52. "An Inverness merchant of the
olden time". William Mackay LLB (ed), T & A Constable, Edinburgh
1915. (NLS ref ABS 278 80(7).
(GLASGOW PAST & PRESENT) Vol II p.460, David Robertson & Co,
Glasgow 1864.
(DELL, for SRO References) Glasgow Register of Companies to 1776,
composed and edited by Richard F Dell, City Archivist Glasgow
Corporation 1971 (Mitchell Library).

(BIGWOOD) The Vice-Admiral Court of Argyll, Processes, etc, 1685-1825 by Frank Bigwood (ed), 2001, Flat B, the Lodge, 2 East Rd, North Berwick EH39 4HN. (£5.00).
Argyll & Bute Archives reference: 1732 AC 20/2/4.
(WILKINS) Various smuggling publications, especially concerning links with the Isle of Man, by Frances Wilkins. Eg The Smuggling Story of the Northern Shores (1995) and Strathclyde's Smuggling Story (1992), Booklist from Wyre Forest Press, 8 Mill Close, Blakedown, Kidderminster, Worcs DY10 3NQ.
(CULLEN) Smuggling and the Ayrshire Economic Boom of the 1760s and 1770s by Prof L M Cullen. Ayrshire Monographs No 14, Pub Sept 1994 by Ayrshire Archaeological & Natural History Society.

Sources Consulted
A Maritime History of Scotland 1650-1790 by Eric J Graham, Tuckwell Press, East Linton, East Lothian EH40 3DG 2002.
Maritime Scotland by Brian Lavery. B T Batsford/Historic Scotland 2001.
Perspectives on the running of contraband cargoes between Ireland and the Scottish Highlands in the mid-eighteenth century by Fiona Macdonald, Scottish Gaelic Studies, Vol XVII 1996, pp 221-238.
Clyde Coast Smuggling or a hundred years of Clyde cutters and smugglers, by J R D Campbell, (45 pp booklet) St Maura Press 1994.
Customs, tobacco and smuggling in South Western Scotland by Sybil M Jack
In Scottish History Volume 2, June 1994, pp 52-75.
The Royal Burgh of Inveraray by Alexander Fraser, St Andrew Press, Edinburgh, 1977.
A Glasgow Miscellany. The Tobacco Period in Glasgow, 1707-75. By Gourlay. (Mitchell Library, Glasgow, Reference G 941 435 GOU).
Scottish Society 1707-1830 by Christopher A Whatley, 2000.
People & Society in Scotland 1760-1830, (Ed) Devine & Mitchison, 1988.
Clanship Commerce & the House of Stuart 1603-1788 by Allan Macinnes.
Portrait of Argyll and Southern Hebrides by David Graham-Campbell, 1978.
Oban – Past & Present, by Charles Hunter, 1995.